EBURY PRESS

UNPARENTING

Reema Ahmad is a neurolinguistic programming life coach and is also a mental space psychologist, and she works in the area of healing from trauma, abuse, violence and relationship issues.

Reema co-edited an anthology of women's work called *Of Dry Tongues and Brave Hearts* with Semeen Ali. It was published by Red River Press in 2022. She is a poet and has also written articles for online publications like Scroll, Vice, Daily O and Live Mint. She is also a TedX and Josh Talks speaker.

Reema began her career as a child sexual abuse awareness educator and went on to specialize as a sexuality educator. She then co-founded Candidly, a forum to explore issues of gender, sexuality and media, with her friend Amita Malhotra in 2017.

Reema graduated from LSR, Delhi University. Her schooling and early years were spent in Agra, where she now lives with her parents, her son, two dogs and three cats.

ADVANCE PRAISE FOR *UNPARENTING*

'With this path-breaking, searingly honest and much-needed book, Reema Ahmad tears through the many misconceptions of parenting. So many of us have children because that is considered the next logical step after marriage, without a thought about how to bring up the child. Parenting isn't just about taking care of the child but being aware that we are bringing forth a life on this earth, not a commodity. In her book, Ahmad challenges the preset notions of parenting competencies. With personal examples, she takes us through the steps of treating a child as an equal, being upfront and honest, gentle and understanding and, instead of demanding blind obedience, empathizing with differences. Her tips on how to talk to your child about sex, consent, sexual abuse and body parts will be an invaluable help to everyone who decides to become a parent. She answers each question in a forthright manner, however inconvenient it may be or however embarrassed *you* may be. Parents, if you are finding it difficult to deal with awkward questions, it's time to unparent with Ahmad. I wish this book had been written when I became a parent. I know I would have been a better parent and my children the happier for it'—Rana Safvi, author and historian

'Simultaneously dreamy and pragmatic, a real and honest love song about human relationships'—Saikat Majumdar, novelist, critic and academic

'*Unparenting* covers a gamut of topics such as body acceptance, bullying, generational trauma, loss, divorce, sexuality and various other important issues that many parents tend to sweep under the rug, simply because they don't have the vocabulary or the material to understand children and themselves better and create a safe enough space for both of them. That makes this book a must-read for parents, but an even more important read for those who are pondering over the idea of parenthood in the chaotic world of today'—Andaleeb Wajid, author

'A parenting book that doesn't presume to preach but attempts to explore together with the reader, holding hands. Sensitively written, with an honesty that is often hard to come by, it handles serious issues with the lightest touch. An important book for our times, and indeed, for all times to come'—Zehra Naqvi, journalist and author

'Reema Ahmad has always been the guru to turn to when wrestling with life's many perplexing moments. She always has the sagest advice measured with equal amounts of humour and long-term insights. Her book is just that. A Bible to keep next to you as children run riot over your life and well-being. Gobsmackingly honest and chatty in its approach, this is just the kind of friend one needs as we all grow in our lives—both the parents and the children! A treasure of a book indeed'—Nazia Erum, author

unPARENTING

Sharing
Awkward Truths
with **Curious Kids**

REEMA AHMAD

EBURY
PRESS

An imprint of Penguin Random House

EBURY PRESS

USA | Canada | UK | Ireland | Australia
New Zealand | India | South Africa | China

Ebury Press is part of the Penguin Random House group of companies
whose addresses can be found at global.penguinrandomhouse.com

Published by Penguin Random House India Pvt. Ltd
4th Floor, Capital Tower 1, MG Road,
Gurugram 122 002, Haryana, India

First published in Ebury Press by Penguin Random House India 2022

10 9 8 7 6 5 4 3 2 1

The views and opinions expressed in this book are the author's own and the
facts are as reported by her which have been verified to the extent possible,
and the publishers are not in any way liable for the same.

ISBN 9780143447764

Typeset in Minion Pro by MAP Systems, Bengaluru, India

www.penguin.co.in

*For Ammi and Abba, who taught me
to have courage in the
bleakest of times*

For Imaad

*I did not know how to
Love you enough
Or how to love you right
When you were given to me
Eyes shut tight to a new world
Without water
Skin pink and wrinkled like
A shorn rabbit's
You did not feel mine
Or born of me
You were a creature of want
I learned to respond to
Watchful and diligent
Trying very hard to be
Something that did not
Come naturally to me
Being a good mother
Over the years I have often waited
For one hour one day
Unpeopled by the constant strain
Of your demands
Your thoughts your ideas
The reality of you
Seemed to have eclipsed
The idea of me*

A full lunar eclipse
Which left everything else
Seeming invisible
And now that I have
That hour that day that week
Of long-desired solitude
I rush to fill it
With people
With places
With things
Because the haunting silence
Of this new truth
My life without
Your persistent presence
My body unadorned by your
Boy arms
Is too much to bear
What scares me more is that
Some day
Like today
You will go on being happy
Without me
That you will learn to be
Whole without me
I, who was never again whole
After I gave birth
To you.

You are my reason for trying to stay alive and sane.
Love always,
Amma

Contents

Introduction

I became a reluctant, unprepared, young mother at the age of twenty-five. My parenting journey has been one of learning and not teaching, following and not leading, and more often than not, living in doubt. Why should I presume that my doubts and anxieties as a parent will be of any use to you? Perhaps because the one perspective that has continued to save me from taking the moral high ground as a parent and, therefore, losing my connection with my child, is constantly reminding myself of what it was like to feel lost, misunderstood and angry as a child. That is the feeling that informs all of my better responses to any situation I find myself in as a millennial parent.

I believe the fact that I sometimes try to think about how I would feel if I was my son in that moment, somehow brings us closer to each other. That is the perspective I want to share through this book. I am no expert; I falter all the time, but the one thing I am, is aware—of my shortcomings, of the ways in which I need to evolve as a parent and an individual.

Awareness, or persisting with it, is perhaps the very purpose of my life, maybe of this book too.

Parenting has become a science in itself, in this day and age. Everywhere you look, there are stacks and stacks of books available to get that one thing right—the art of becoming the perfect parent—the one who knows everything, does everything right and never fails at the demanding, exacting job that it is. And yet, behind this incessant hankering for perfection lies a barely perceptible sense of inadequacy, of unpreparedness for something as profound as caring for another human being. This book seeks to explore this vulnerability, this apprehension, which comes naturally to parents. To put it simply, nothing really prepares you for parenting. The only way to learn is through sharing openly.

So much of what we do as parents and who we become in the act of parenting is passed on to us culturally and socially from our own parents and families. And in the Indian milieu, there's unlimited advice on what to feed a child, how to structure their routines and get them to perform better, to be more obedient. But when you look at the grey areas, the difficult questions that require more input from one's self and more exploration of our own biases as adults, we draw a blank. There are no easy answers on how to talk to our children about keeping themselves safe from sexual abuse, no manuals on how to safely explore and express their sexuality, how to recognize unhealthy relationships and explore personal ambiguities with the intention of learning, at least not enough material that seems to *talk* to us without the use of big terms, jargon and fancy language.

Perhaps there are no chatty manuals on these subjects because they defy easy categorization. And yet, our experiences with our bodies, and a sense of our sexual preferences are important. Our responses to media and culture as children greatly shape our behaviour and responses as adults. What we watch, hear and read is absorbed by our children too and they're not prepared like we think they are. There's so much out there—violence, anger, betrayal, grief—everything reaches them just as it reaches us.

This book is not a manual about how to decode everything that we absorb. It is simply an honest attempt at exploring parental attitudes towards addressing sensitive issues with children—attitudes that have been ingrained in us through culture and habit. In a way, this book is about 'unparenting'—freeing ourselves from notions of how we're *supposed* to react or behave in tricky situations and simply learning how to put the child first. And these situations don't just have to do with the body or a growing child's sexuality. They could be about anything that we didn't really think about when we had a child; like bullying or how to explain death to a child or how to respond to questions about divorce and relationships.

Such situations are often fleeting, yet significant—needing patience, time to pause and reflect. So much so, that our entire life's experiences up to that moment somehow percolate through and create our response. Sometimes we need to block certain experiences from filtering through, and at other times we have to let memory flow through us freely like a river, never dammed.

It's never easy to know exactly when to do what; and I share here only my experiences as a mother, teacher and trainer. And more often than I would have liked, my own memories of what I felt as a child. Observing myself, my parents and my friends who are parents, I have seen a distinct pattern emerge and take shape. In most alarming or awkward incidents, shock, denial, anger and confusion are the foremost feelings of a parent when he or she discovers that a child has overstepped a boundary or has been harmed in some way. Fear and anxiety hijack the problem at hand and all our focus shifts to 'controlling' the situation rather than reflecting on appropriate responses. Offering reassurances and security to a harried child and understanding what he or she is going through somehow takes a backseat.

In this book, I have tried to make that much-needed shift from anxiety to exploration, from fear to understanding, and from anger to acceptance. Through the reactions, responses and questions of a growing boy, I have attempted to explore my role as a parent trying to raise a self-aware and respectful child. Together, we seek to comprehend and value questioning as an important tool of discovery. In doing so, we attempt to change the dynamics of what is acceptable or unacceptable, what is shameful or worthy of respect, what is wrong or right and most importantly, what is needed for healthy growth— not just physically, but also emotionally and sexually.

In the three years it took for me to write this book, the pandemic came and stayed. I went from being a very confident mother who thought she knew a lot, to crumbling as a parent—to the extent that I stopped writing for more than a year. To write about parenting felt so hypocritical when I myself was struggling. As all known structures of industry, work, medicine and education shattered and transformed, changing our children with them, I experienced uncertainty like never before, as did millions of others.

The mutating, shape-shifting virus has shown us that we barely know anything about the nature of life and death. We may like to believe that we have all the cures and answers, and that is reflected in the way we use technology to monitor everything: from our heart rate, to the number of steps we take, to the number of millimetres the arctic glaciers melt in a day. We install cameras that monitor our kids and their nannies, we count calories and edit our social-media feeds to appear woke and trending. And yet, we are helpless in the face of larger forces like the coronavirus. It wriggles out of our control.

Parenting can't be controlled either. We can read manuals and books (like this one) and feel smug that we know *how to do* everything. We can plan schools, life insurance, colleges and finances but we don't know how and when life can derail all of our plans. Our children's destinies are not regulated by our plans. And children themselves teach us that we know very little about anything. With their free spirits, their wilfulness, their wild ways, their inherent need to challenge us and their ability to find joy in the smallest of things, they constantly remind us that we could do better by learning from them and not the other way round.

But what I *have* learned through the pandemic and my ongoing parenting journey is that being flexible, open and curious really helps me keep in sync with the times. Perhaps this is what I hope to achieve for myself through this book; the ability to hold the identity of a parent with a light hand on the reins as I return, time and again, to not knowing, and being eminently comfortable with that ignorance. And perhaps in doing so, I can change to a being who is humble, curious and still in the process of learning, a presence for my child, as opposed to someone trying to fix and mould him. As you walk this path with me through this book, I hope that happens for you too.

Warmly,
Reema

The Beginning

Although this book was intended to explore the quirkier, uncomfortable, often comical bits of parenting, I believe no part can be fully covered until we try and uncover the basis of the whole. This section, therefore, might be unexpected and perhaps a little intimidating, unlike (hopefully) the rest of the book. But I need you to stay; not for you and me, but for all the unborn and extant children of this world. Please walk with me because the words on these pages don't belong merely in the stories of those who live in poverty and strife, or in the annals of research manuals and government reports. They also belong in the stories of people like us—aware, concerned and educated parents who write, buy and read books on parenting so that they may become better at performing the everyday miracle of child rearing. They belong in 'fun' and light books too because the biggest part of the journey called parenting is learning to navigate fear; fear of the process, of the future and of the darkness that resides in all of us.

* * *

Origins

Like a great storm
we shook
the tree of life
down to the hiddenmost
fibres of its roots
and you appear now
singing in the foliage
in the highest branch
that with you we reach.*

—Pablo Neruda, *'The Son'**

Nothing carves itself on our visceral memory like pain; it leaves the deepest scars—the rich purples of throbbing bruises intertwined with the white skeins of our mind. I remember the day after my son was born as vividly as the harsh fibres of the kilim rug beneath my feet right now. I had been trying to sit up and feed the baby for two hours. Sharp spikes of pain emanated from the ten stitches I had needed after an episiotomy. I didn't recognize my body or mind any more. Every pore was a gnashing scream. I gritted my teeth while two nurses tried to extract milk from my swollen nipples with syringes because the baby wouldn't latch on. My older sister wiped the sweat off my face and neck. It was the coldest week of January that year. She looked like she would gladly switch places with me at this moment. And there I was, my body half bared, bereft of all dignity—the fuzzy, maternal happiness

---

*Neruda, Pablo, 'The Son', https://genius.com/Pablo-neruda-the-son-annotated

portrayed in the Johnson's Baby Powder Ad a very far cry from the reality of my humiliating situation. All I wanted was to give up and go to sleep. Anything, but this, I whimpered to myself; *anything*!

I also remember the father of my child walking into the room at that moment. 'Someone is waiting to see the baby,' he told me.

'I can't,' I groaned. 'I'm trying to feed the baby and all I can think of is sleep. Please tell them to wait.'

Something in him buckled, exploded and splintered across the room, slamming into me in waves that still resound. 'You can't even feed the baby. It's been two hours! You're not the only woman who has ever given birth,' he almost screamed.

In that moment, I realized just how unprepared he was, how completely at sea; his anxiety roiled within him until it spewed forth as blind rage, inundating us all. It wasn't like he didn't care. This was the same man who had helped me walk to the bathroom that morning. The man who had helped me change and clean myself, who would later try and learn to change and feed our son and rock him to sleep. But at that kairotic moment, when we were being tested, both of us failed.

All I could think of was my pain, my need, my discomfort. And all he could do was expect to be heard. As the days passed, we learned to mechanically do what was needed of us, but where was that joy that everyone spoke of, where was that overwhelming rush of parental emotion? He was proud and tender in lapses, but mostly he paced, ranted and impulsively cracked open nuts while everyone around him tried not to scream. I was faking my joy at best. Hadn't we yearned for this?

During labour, the only compassionate nurse in the room had said that the first ones were always a little difficult, the second ones slipped out easily. 'Slip' was not the word

I could get my tongue around during those sixteen hours of excruciating labour, trying to eject a four-kilo baby out of me. Tear was the only word I felt. Like my upper lip was being pulled over my head and I could hear every fibre, every muscle, stretch and rip. The other rupture was happening inside, quietly creeping in—the enormity of bringing a life into this world and nurturing it. My heart almost splitting free from my body in trepidation. I felt the wrench of confidence from spirit, assurance from resolve and fear of everything else that remained; a fear that overshadowed the miracle of birth. I was desperately afraid.

With the possibility of life, I had also let in the possibility of death, of sorrow and of complete and abject failure. We had been somewhat prepared to welcome the joy, but of its dark twin, we hadn't had a clue. It wasn't surprising that we were unprepared, like most young parents are; what was shocking was that we doubted whether we even wanted this, that we had *unthinkingly* and selfishly decided to undertake the monumental task of raising and caring for another human being.

* * *

Long before we learn to climb out of childhood and unlearn all that we naturally know in order to become adults, the world begins to spin a silvery web around us. This web is a sparkling tinsel of stories, songs and lore that lure us into believing in dreams, much like the wind chimes lull us to sleep. And before we know it, the promise held out by this web becomes an undeniable need—like a soporific security blanket, bringing us comfort and relief. What is this enchanting, terrible music? What does it want us to do? What does it want us to be?

'May you be the mother of a hundred sons,' whispers an ancient Hindu blessing to young brides through the ages. 'May you never be *miskeen* (poor),' goes the customary Libyan greeting after each salaam, where being 'poor' is not the lack of wealth and riches, but the lack of progeny.

As my father would often laughingly tell us, even having four children can invite sympathetic laments of '*Wallahmiskeen* (alas, you poor one)!' from well-meaning Libyans. From times immemorial, long before the origin of word or song, culture and creed has exhorted us to reproduce, to bring forth life into this world so we may feel 'complete'. As ancient fertility rites and rituals, modern cures and most recently, the much-sought-after artificial reproductive miracles would have us believe, procreation is the foremost thing that can bring us joy. And we blindly believe all of this at the cost of reason, at the cost of psychological and physical pain, at the cost of the well-being of those future children themselves who are custom designed by self-absorbed parents to serve as props in this elaborate drama of lonely lives. We have carried around this delusion for centuries, as if leaving our biological imprint on the physical history of this planet could make us immortal after death and fulfilled while alive.

Maybe we need these stories, cures and rituals as crutches when we embark on the precarious journey of inhabiting this planet as a species. We need the magic of lore to propel us into the future and let our genes lead us. Modern science has proven that the human race is wired to procreate with a compulsion so strong that it is difficult to ignore. And, with time, the establishment of the family as the foundation and sign of a civilized society has further strengthened that urge. The myth that a union between a man and a woman is complete only when they create offspring, further drives this bizarre ancient need.

But why do I speak as if creating children or needing them is something unnatural? Why do I call this need terrible? Especially when I have written this book on parenting, when I am a mother myself? I feel that in this rush to propagate our species, to achieve fulfilment and immortality, to feel whole and happy, we have forgotten something crucial to the survival of the very thing we need—the clarity to want to reproduce not because we feel we need children, but because we *want* them.

Perhaps you disagree with me but bear with me a while. I have spent a lot of time teaching children, and the adults around them, the means and ways to stay safe and happy. Time and again I have been confronted by the fact that very few parents think deeply about what a child really needs beyond the basic requirements of food, clothing and shelter. When we decide to have a child, or have one unwittingly, we pay very little attention to the life that is yet unborn. We may ponder deeply about what it will mean to us, but mostly we envision a life where our routines, the rhythm of our lives and our circumstances will determine how that child lives its life. What we don't realize is the fact that the unborn child has *no* say in the matter about the beginning of its existence and none at all during its life on earth. It exists simply because we thought it was the right thing to do at that moment in time or because we were in love or married and our families wanted us to have a family. Does that tiny, beautiful, incredible, individual life exist because you want it to exist, because you're ready and *prepared* to welcome and nurture it with presence and joy? Or does it exist because you think it is something that must be done or simply because there was a condom 'accident'?

We need answers to these questions to understand what happened to the hardened mini-adults and the delinquent and traumatized, the suicidal and depressed, the violent and vindictive children, so easily labelled as 'bad influences'. They populate our news headlines, school classrooms and therapy clinics. We warn our children to stay away from 'them'. Yet they were born innocent too. We need to probe deeper into our own patterns of need and neglect as parents that create these 'bad' children who never really grow up. They attempt to pass as adults all their lives.

There's a passage in Rosalind Miles's path-breaking book, *The Children We Deserve*,* that first made me think about how limited we are in the way we obsess about our problems as parents. And this was when I was already considered to be an old hand, mothering an eleven-year-old. It says:

> . . . there is an uneasy sense that the children of today are very different from the young of times past: more sophisticated yet less responsible, more out of hand yet more demanding, more sensation seeking and more drug abusing, more delinquent and more dangerous than ever before. The classic adult reaction from anorexic daughters to joy-riding adults is to ask, 'What have we done to deserve this?' Yet could not these children make the same demand of us, with even more natural justice?

Meaning that, is it fair of us to blame every obstacle we face in rearing children on the children themselves, their temperaments, their schools, the neighbourhood kids or that old scapegoat—*western culture and media*? Is it fair, that

---

*Miles, Rosalind, *The Children We Deserve: Love and Hate in the Making of the Family*, Harper Collins, 1994. Non-fiction.

at every horrific headline that talks of seven-year-old drug
dealers and twelve-year-old rapists, we clutch each other in
terror and wail, 'What is the world coming to?'

As Miles says, should we not be asking ourselves, 'What
have *we* done to let it come to this?' Where are we going
wrong, where is our blind spot that makes it difficult for us to
look at children as individuals and not little robots that need
to be controlled and disciplined? What are our limitations
as men and women or non-binary parents that limit our
understanding of, and responses to, the needs of children?
Children are born powerless, innocent and harmless. If they
destroy themselves and others, if they fall prey to violence and
abuse, then surely, their circumstances are a reflection of the
society they live in. Even if we look beyond these children
who have been cruelly treated and severely abused, these
experiences then manifesting in their own behaviour, children
are routinely subjected to fear, punishment, deprivation and
neglect.

And no one intervenes.

Why?

* * *

Faltering

(*All names in this section have been changed*)

An affluent, well-educated acquaintance of mine called me
one day last year. She has always been very supportive of my
work and my writing in the three years that I have known
her. We chatted a few times, and at one point, I tutored
her son for a few months; an adorable child with sparkling
eyes and a smile that was the joy of my class at summer
camp. I couldn't help but feel horrified at what his mother

wanted to discuss with me that day. Her son's innocent face swam before my mind's eye for hours after we spoke. This little child was cared for at home by a young man not more than seventeen while both his parents went to work. There's nothing extraordinary or deplorable about that, lots of parents need to employ help because they simply need to work. And this young man was known to the family, his father had worked for them for years. That afternoon my friend told me that her then four-year-old son had reported being touched inappropriately by the help a few times while the couple were out late at night. They had counselled the help and installed cameras in the house for better protection but had chosen to let him stay on after he apologized and promised not to repeat the behaviour. This happens too. Sometimes circumstances force us into a corner, and we are pushed to make very difficult choices out of sheer necessity, hoping that our faith will not be abused.

That is not the whole story. Recently, my friend called me again to share that they had started leaving their second infant son in the help's care as well when they went out in the evenings or nights and that the older child had again reported of being touched by the help. The mother was worried that the help might abuse the infant and the baby might not even be able to report it. She wanted me to advise her about what she should do. Should she fire the help? It was a difficult thing to do because of the family dynamics involved. Should she stop going out? She'd have to hire someone eventually because she couldn't always be present at home. Could her older child be lying about this? The help had been soundly thrashed and swore blind that he hadn't touched the child. Her husband felt that it wasn't really all that serious; furthermore they had no other alternative.

It took me a while to absorb the fact that she was even asking me these questions *despite* the history involved.

This account is by no means an attempt on my part to shame that lady or make her feel inadequate as a mother. She's a kind, caring human being and I'm sure she does the best she can as a parent, like all of us. I have been guilty of grave indifference towards my child on many occasions and I'm still learning how to be more aware and attuned to need and danger. The point is that this is a parent who is educated and aware, who knows about abuse awareness and the effects of sexual abuse on children. These are parents who made the choice to let a potential abuser (who himself was in dire need of guidance) stay on to care for their little sons in their absence. How could this happen? Why did they not think it could have been disastrous for both their children and they could have been violently hurt and deeply traumatized? They loved and cared for their children, they provided for them the best they could and yet it took repeated incidents for them to understand how to put their children first. Why?

Why did it take me to be harsh and direct with her, telling her that if she wanted the safety and well-being of her children, the help needed to go at any cost—be it at the cost of familial disturbance, the cost of evenings out, the cost of less income and a diminished comfort level in their lifestyle. The help needed to go, and he needed to be reported and counselled. Why did it have to come to this for her to make that call to me? Why did she even need me to tell her something that every parent should instinctively know? She did the sensible thing in the end, but it took so long, so dangerously long. Some parents never make that call. Some parents don't pay heed to a child's voice and a few simply look away. Not because they don't care, but because they simply do not comprehend the practical and emotional cost of caring for a child when they *chose* to have the child. Or because they had no way of preparing themselves for the many familial, cultural and social constraints that they would have to navigate, and sometimes rebel against, while rearing a child. I don't think many of us think through all these ramifications before we decide to become parents. Consequently, we end up making decisions (or not making them) that endanger our children, sometimes fatally. This couple believed they were equipped to become parents, they thought they were ready, like most of us who imagine we're going to be *competent* parents; just as I had assumed—until I took a good hard look at myself.

* * *

Little Muneer is now a grown man. He married his girlfriend of three years in the teeth of opposition from both sides of the family. They moved into a small apartment in a new city, excited to begin their life together. Let's call his wife Zara. Muneer and Zara are very happy to be together but, in a few months, something begins to unravel in their relationship. Muneer is very possessive, too possessive. He watches Zara all the time; he holds on to her as they sleep and she finds it suffocating. He lashes out at her if she's ever late returning home after work; he throws a hissy fit if things are not done exactly the way he wants them done. When Zara tries to reason with Muneer, he get defensive and says she doesn't love or care for him. Zara is understandably confused and hurt; she always feels smothered, limited and guilty.

This is not love—she can hear this phrase scrolling like tickertape in the back of her head all the time. She tries to ignore it. But he does love her, doesn't he? He massages her feet when she's tired, he buys her little presents, he is passionate and finds her beautiful in every way, he even cares for her when she's ill. Yet the growing unease fills the spaces between them.

One evening, Muneer angrily flings the surprise meal that Zara has ordered in, in the hope of raising their spirits a bit. The food plasters the walls of their pristine home. They have a huge argument. Later that night, Muneer pushes Zara out of their little flat. He continues to throw and break things in his rage while Zara bangs on the door, pleading with him to stop. The neighbour finds her outside her door in the morning, a crumpled, frightened, tear-stained heap; utterly alone in a new city.

Six months and a brief separation later, Muneer is in therapy. Urged by family and friends to mend things between them, Muneer and his wife seek help to understand his sudden outbursts and dangerously unreasonable behaviour. After a lot of probing, medication and hypnotherapy, childhood neglect, abuse and violence are identified as the causes of Muneer's aggressive behaviour and the reason for all the trauma he has inflicted on Zara. He is deeply remorseful and wants to make amends. In one of the joint sessions with their therapist, Zara listens with tears in her eyes as Muneer describes an incident from his childhood that has been seared into his memory:

'I was six years old. I used to walk to nursery school and back. It wasn't very far from home, I didn't mind. Ammi was busy, she had a lot to do, she was a professor in the university; Abba was busy too. I remember it was summer, right before the holidays began. My shirt used to stick to my back on my way home. Ammi would sprinkle Nycil powder on my back in the mornings, but the itching persisted, nevertheless. It was very hot, and I stopped to buy a lolly from the ice- cream vendor near our house. I still remember the sharp tang of orange melting in my mouth.

'The melting lolly dripped on to my shirt, my hands and face. Everything was sticky and I was a mess. Ammi was going to be hopping mad. When I got home, I found our front door locked from the inside. It was never locked during the day. I stood ringing the bell for a long time. I could hear Ammi moving around inside. I called out to her, but she didn't open the door. It was evening when she finally opened it. I think I must have stood outside, ringing the bell and crying for at least three hours. Ammi didn't speak to me that evening. I was fifteen minutes late. Fifteen minutes. Ammi loved me. But she also broke me; sometimes with her silence and often with the rusted bathroom wiper, Abba's belt, anything that was handy. Once she hit me with a scalding *chimti* (tong). I still have the scar. The next morning, she made my favourite halwa. Abba loved me too, but he never intervened when Ammi hit me.' Muneer breaks down and weeps for a long time. The therapist passes him a box of tissues and makes notes in Muneer's files.

The above passages may seem like a story out of a Bollywood movie, but they are a glimpse into the reality of emotional and physical abuse that happens in countless households across the world. I know the two people mentioned above. I know their story because I have seen it unfold before me. I also know the story of that angry, depressed, tortured mother who forever changed the meaning of love for that little child. She didn't know how to love herself, and in her outrage and grief, she passed on her scars to her child who further passed them on to his wife. Would you say Muneer was a brute? Who made him that way? Was his mother an unfeeling monster? Who made her that way? Who was responsible? All I can say is that, when we understand and practise parental love as the freedom to punish and care at whim and without control, we pass on only our fractured sense of belonging to our children. And these children then pass on this generational trauma, anger and grief to their children; a devastating legacy of parental love that is confusing at best and violent at its worst. How many of us have the resources, courage, support and commitment to work on our childhood wounds and unlearn hurtful behaviour patterns before we have children? Very few. For most couples, childhood relationship scars emerge sharply when they enter into marriages. That is when all of our suppressed pain raises its ugly head because, since our childhood, we have not had the opportunity to live so closely with another human being. How many of us seek healing and resolution when this happens?

* * *

Mariam has four children. She lives in a small town in North India with her husband Danny. The ages of Mariam and Danny's four children fall between two years (the youngest, Annie) to the seventeen-year-old Asif, who is the oldest. But there's really not that much of a difference between the oldest and the youngest except for the size of their bodies.

Asif cannot read or speak, or sit up, eat or walk on his own. All he can do is lie all day long in whatever position he has been put in until his exhausted mother finds the time to turn him on to his side, or wipe the spit dribbling from his mouth, or feed him when she has the time. The two other children between Asif and Annie are not much different. Despite countless visits to doctors after the birth of each child, Mariam and her husband don't have a diagnosis for the condition of their children. It's a disease where the child loses all movement in the limbs and brain development ceases after the age of one. But the children keep growing physically.

'It's a curse,' says Mariam. And yet many in her community would censure her for saying this.

Mariam and Danny are perpetually exhausted. If there were a word that could accurately describe the condition between death and dying, it would perhaps summarize the helplessness and drudgery this couple goes through in their every waking second. Neither of them gets more than one hour of sleep per night and despite all the help they get from kind relatives and friends, they are at their wits' end. When social workers visit the family, the parents tell them they wish there were a way to put all four children to sleep.

To an outsider this might seem cruel or even barbaric, but for someone who lives with the reality of four disabled children who are growing in body and not in mind or function, it is not surprising they feel this way. Of course, one might ask the usual questions—did the children get any treatment? were they taken to any special childcare units? have people donated their help and money to aid the couple in their struggle with the children? The answer to all of these is yes. The family's story was covered in several major newspapers a few years ago and a lot of people offered medical, physical and monetary help. It did make things a little easier for the family, like the availability of better food and someone to take over the changing and bathing of the children when the money allowed it. Even so, it is not hard to imagine how difficult it must be to raise four children who cannot even wipe their own faces. The reality is that as the children grow in body, things will only get worse. It will become increasingly difficult to care for them the way they need to be cared for. These children have no future, no quality of life and no hope. And yet, their parents chose to have more children even after it was abundantly clear that there was something seriously wrong with the first two.

I wonder if things could have been different for Mariam and Danny if a doctor had advised them not to have any more children after the first or maybe the second. Or if they could have taken different decisions had some doctor prescribed tests that could detect abnormalities when Mariam was pregnant each time. There are so many things that one could wonder about and I have even wondered why Mariam and Danny continued trying to have babies when they had seen what Nature had chosen for them. Could they not have opted for birth-control measures, so easily available today, to put a stop to bringing forth human beings into this world who would only know suffering and pain? Perhaps they would have, had their religion and culture not taught them that to even think of cutting short a life divinely ordained is a sin (even if that life is worse than that of any sentient being on the planet), that to interfere with God's work would be the same as actively seeking hell in the afterlife.

Those who believe in religion and God could say that children are God's gifts and that nobody has the right to refuse a gift. But how much choice did these suffering children really have? Their parents made that choice, perhaps, believing in the archaic notion that children are divine gifts that cannot be refused. They could not or did not fathom what it would mean for all of them later. When Mariam finds the time to pray now, she cries and pleads for the pain to end. People who sometimes come to visit and gape at her children often tell her that this is her karma, a punishment for sins committed by her or her children in a past life. Some tell her that this is a divine test and that she must have faith that God will provide. What they do not tell her is that what her God will *not* be able to provide for

Mariam, and for millions like her in the world, is a reliable, cheap form of birth prevention that can reduce the trauma and pain of so many pregnancies that are neither wanted nor desired. How many parents are ready for a life like this? How many parents who have to care for very sick children have the emotional, financial and physical capacity to actually be able to do them justice?

People who rave against abortion and birth-control measures are often those who have never had to struggle with raising a child alone, or care for a physically or emotionally impaired child with very little help, or deal with the aftermath of an unwanted pregnancy at a young age, completely unprepared and unaided.

The gift of life that two parents receive is divine indeed, but you tell me, dear reader, should Mariam and Danny be grateful for the great suffering they have been put through? Would their life have been easier if they had looked for methods that could help them control and contain the ongoing battle that is their life, not to mention sparing their children the immense suffering and indignity they have had to endure all their lives?

When I first read Mariam and Danny's story two years ago, I was emotionally troubled by the prospect of death for these children who could not speak for themselves. But, when I visited this poor, destitute, struggling family, I had no doubt whatsoever in my mind about what was more sinful—keeping these children alive in such inhumane conditions or their parents' wish to let them slide into a gentler state of nonexistence. Earlier last month, I read a report saying that Asif had passed away and that his younger brother was also showing signs of speedy deterioration. It was only a matter of time before the remaining two followed the fate of their older siblings. Can this painful existence even be called *life*?

There are only two words that come to mind whenever I think of Asif, Annie, the other two children, and their hapless parents—*what if?*

* * *

Looking within

> *The way I see the world, we are constantly at risk from the people we love the most.*
> *They, after all, are the only people who can do us serious damage, a damage that lasts forever.*

—Jennifer Johnston

I tell you these grim stories because it is important for us to realize what we are doing with children; it is crucial we examine whether we are even *capable* of bringing up healthy, well-adjusted children. Behind the social rhetoric that encourages young couples to build a family lives an entirely different reality. One in four children in the world are destined to live below the poverty line, hundreds will suffer from lack of proper emotional and physical care, thousands will give in to drink, drugs or delinquency. In the global recession, child pornography remained one of the few booming industries. These truths don't just reflect the lives of the economically weaker section of global society, they reflect our reality everywhere. The question therefore is, why do we bring children into the world, knowing what lies in store?

The first step towards getting the children we deserve is in having children we really, truly want with all our hearts. The second, is to prepare ourselves- emotionally physically and financially—to take care of them. There are too many babies born to those who have not progressed beyond the assumption that having a baby is the next inevitable stage of life's journey after leaving school, getting a job and getting married. We need to question this assumption if we are to progress towards achieving the children we deserve and giving them the love, life and attention that is their indisputable birth right.

* * *

Of Mothers

In order to parent in a way that befits this gift of life, we need to examine all the social and cultural traditions that have been handed down to us as incontestable tenets. Take for example the ideal of motherhood that has been upheld as the apotheosis of female existence for centuries. Women are brainwashed into believing that motherhood is an inevitable, inalienable right, duty or necessity; but does that hold true for every woman? *The best and happiest children come from mothers who chose this role of their own free will.* How many mothers can honestly say that? How many women are even in a position to choose, without some kind of familial or social pressure? I know I wasn't in that position and I do believe that has some bearing on my struggle to mother instinctively. I have always had to struggle to choose the needs of my child before my own and perhaps that has defined that process, that learning, for me so clearly.

History has borne witness to the fate of those women who failed to produce heirs as queens and women in power. In most cases, prominent women knew that the continuance of their line, even their survival, depended entirely on the fruits of their womb. To this day, women are not spared the indignity of being labelled barren, and are often evicted from households or relegated to being secondary wives when their husbands remarry because they've been unable to bear children. Women have always had to face the brunt of society's taunts for being unwilling or unable to produce children. If we are honest with ourselves, we will see that women who are compelled or brainwashed into breeding in order to *complete* their identity of the archetypal woman, will not be fully prepared or be able to look after these children with wholehearted willingness, love and warmth.

As working women in the post-modern world, most of us are familiar with the anxiety and duality that confronts us as we are harried to balance both home and family with the added pressure of achieving perfection. Most of us end up resenting our children or our careers at some point, as it becomes harder to do justice to both. But we're not allowed to even acknowledge this fact to our own selves, much less say it out loud, because it will be mistaken for lack of maternal love or the modern bane that supposedly afflicts women— *selfishness.* I do believe that resentment cannot but colour the affection and attention that our children deserve. As human beings we are limited in many ways and it is deeply unfair to expect women to achieve impeccability in everything they do; be it in being wives or mothers.

Motherhood often entails full-time self-sacrifice by the mother and any sacrifice has a very short shelf life. The whole concept of motherhood reduces women to a caricature, a full-time provider of all of the infant's needs. Women routinely suffer from a loss of self and an onslaught of fear and diffidence when they have children. What is even more unjust is the fact that almost *nobody* prepares them for this role. Young mothers often find themselves at the mercy of 'expert' and condescending relatives who're confident they know more about any baby than its own mother could ever be expected to know. When young mothers need support and encouragement they are often bullied and intimidated. Very few fathers and extended family step in to support young mothers in the all-consuming, self-abnegating job that is caring for a newborn.

It is no wonder then that mothers often find themselves depressed, lonely and at a loss about what to do with their children or how to make sense of their drastically changed bodies and lives. And, with modern lifestyles and nuclear families that are far removed from the ready availability of relatives, neighbours and community, mothering has become even lonelier. Postpartum depression is very common in women who did not want children in the first place or were not wholly prepared for it. They often end up inadvertently resenting or putting their children at risk. Even in women who were ready, the sheer biological upheaval of pregnancy and labour can lead to postpartum depression, which makes it very hard for the mother to enjoy mothering, especially in the first few months. This may seem like an outrageous proposition to a culture that is wholly given to venerating motherhood, but unfortunately, it is true.

And God forbid if something were to go wrong! Blame is heaped on the mother:

No breastfeeding? The mother is lazy and vain.

No potty training in time? The mother is inept.

Fussy toddler at the table? The mother is inattentive and too busy to care.

Too much screen time? The mother values her career more than her child.

Two maids to manage the children? What kind of a mother does that?

Is all this blame fair?

We're all guilty of judging mothers, even our own mothers, without recognizing the fact that parenting is not the job of one individual alone. As the old saying goes:

. . . it takes a village to raise a child.

Mothers and fathers, families, schools, media, culture, neighbours and neighbourhoods—all these together make our children what they are. To have the children we deserve we must empower mothers, not intimidate them, offer help and support, not censure and blame.

Just as we are never allowed, or encouraged, to question the construct of becoming mothers, we are also never encouraged to question the very concept of motherhood; to re-examine how we were treated as children. To us our mothers were infallible (and fathers too, for that matter). But mothers are not angels, even at their best. They can't be. To call them 'superheroes' is to feed the myths that only make it easier for these poor women to sacrifice themselves even more.

At their worst, some of the casual, everyday acts of cruelty that mothers are capable of defy belief. Some of you reading this will be familiar with the inexplicable rage outbursts by your mothers or our own monstrous acts of violence against children when we found ourselves at the end of our tether, often unable to think or act in the best interests of the child whose very life we were entrusted with. I, for one, am acutely aware of mine.

Perhaps this book is also a way of recognizing my limitations and trying to expand my sense of responsibility and care. If mothers are divine, as they're made out to be, why do they lose patience, or hit children or lock them in dark rooms? Let us not pretend it doesn't happen, especially in our part of the world. Spare the rod, spoil the child, anyone? We give in to violence and anger because we are either unprepared, without any help, exhausted beyond belief or simply unaware of the demands that motherhood make on a body and mind before we decide to have children.

Then there are women who don't want children—labelled misguided and selfish, vain and non-*sanskaari* (uncultured/ raised without traditional values). They are designated as outcasts, when the truth is they simply don't want children. What they're really suffering from is the failure to live up to the massive cultural expectations of motherhood, not anything abnormal. Most women experience motherhood as a duty and there's nothing wrong with that. The only thing wrong is for society and culture to impose motherhood on women who may not be ready for it. Not all women are cut out for motherhood: in some cases, the woman's biology denies it; in others it might have been a blessing if it had. Yet, as long as we cling to an ideology that sublimates motherhood over every other feminine quality, we shall continue to see unemployed teenagers making the only adult choice open to them, and young women inexorably propelled into maternity whatever their inner reservations or fears. Is this fair to the child born of such compulsion and to the mother giving birth under pressure? As Rosalind Miles beautifully puts it,

> . . . the only time to have a baby is when that new life is calling so strongly to be born that nothing in the world can silence it.

Only the fully aware mother, fully supported in every way, can be a *good enough* mother. As long as women go on having children simply because they have ovaries and uteri, as long as they are encouraged to do so as a part and parcel of their wifely duties and functions and as long as they are then left alone to sift and sieve from the avalanche of familial advice and their own, often suppressed, memories of childhoods, too many children will not get the mothering they truly need and we will continue to see more children suffering, lonely and in pain.

Thankfully, it is becoming increasingly easier for women to make the unconventional choice and openly decide that motherhood is not for them. Many women realize that they are simply not prepared to bring a child into the world and perhaps they're doing the world a favour.

Every child a wanted child, . . .

declared a 1960s birth-control programme in America. If only more young women were able to make motherhood a deliberate choice and not something that is foisted on them by an accidental pregnancy. We can unravel and reject the assumption that every woman can and should opt for motherhood and all she needs to make this decision are her natural maternal instincts. It makes more sense to admit that for motherhood, as for life, each individual needs choice, empowerment and control—all of which are prerequisites to providing children the nurturing they deserve.

* * *

Of Fathers

No one can deny the importance of the mother in the overall development of a healthy and happy individual. Yet despite the universal consensus that the mother is the centre of her child's world, she is not the only participant in its birth and life. In every mythology in the world, except for the Immaculate Conception of Christ, no female makes a baby by herself. Every child must have a father. So what about him?

We take it for granted that to become a mother, a woman learns to set aside her own needs and desires and prioritizes her offspring, almost overnight. But how does a man become a good father, one who can keep his children safe and yet teach them to fly? What does he have to give up, if anything at all? Young couples are often so consumed with each other that they treat each other like children, like babies. But when the real baby arrives, they realize that they have been given someone new to love, someone to whom the mother will be the most wonderful person in the whole world. In contrast, the father has to live with the fact that he will never be number one in anyone's life again. He also has to understand that until he can accept this, he will never be a real father, but will remain forever his partner's eldest child, competing with their children for her attention. And how many of us are not familiar with this? If we're true to ourselves, I'd say almost every woman reading this book has often said this to herself, 'my husband is my biggest baby.' And what does that say about the parental capabilities of that said husband and father?

Until a man has thought about his own ability to cope with fatherhood, to understand all that is required of a father, he cannot be the father that every child needs and deserves. What most men feel when they are suddenly faced with the phenomena of fatherhood is sheer panic. It is a real crisis—it signifies the end of their childhood, the end of carefree days spent with pals and the sudden weight of the care and future of a little human. Most men get little or no space to even acknowledge what they are going through, because to do so would be to bring out their softer feminine side and some men would feel that clashes with their macho self-image. And there are hardly any compassionate spaces where men can talk about the toll that incessant caring for families, giving in to the grind of work and more work, takes on them. Like new motherhood, new fatherhood is similarly surrounded by a conspiracy of denial, of the complete negation of what the reality of fatherhood really is. People congratulate the new father and he beams around, happy to display the living proof of his virility, but no one asks him if he's okay, if he's ready. In all that euphoria, any bad feelings are strictly taboo, and any understanding of what men are really feeling is absent. When a baby is expected, a lot of people show sympathy and concern for the mother and for the existing children, yet no one extends this consideration to a new father who has, up until now, been the prime receiver of his wife's love and care.

Every father flounders with the sudden and near total usurpation of the woman who used to be his partner. She is totally absorbed in the new arrival and quite unable to give him the undivided attention that he was accustomed to. In that sense, the arrival of a child is like a dethroning for the father. A lot of men are trained to not share their feelings with their male friends or family. Most men are socialized to put up a brave front and silently deal with whatever comes their way. All of that suppression and denial comes out somewhere and, in some cases, that dreaded creature is born—the lonely, angry, confused father who is not very different from the child he's supposed to bring up.

Most men are conditioned (one could also say condemned) by society to be the lawmakers and breadwinners and the ones responsible for the stability and prosperity of the family. There are plenty of two-parent families where the father works such long hours that the children never see him except at weekends, and perhaps not even then. How can he then give his children the attention that they do need from him? Until very recently, no more was expected of a father than a distant affection and the monthly pay cheque. And things haven't changed that much; most men expect their wife and children to stay at home and refuse to take any responsibility, except for the financial aspect of homemaking. Looking after children is a brain-damaging activity for most men simply because they're just not trained to physically care for and pay attention to someone on a daily basis. Shared parenting deals a death blow to masculine self-absorption because the man will have to put the children first, and most men don't want that. Most men are too self-involved to even recognize a child's inner turmoil leave alone help the child uncover and overcome it.

From an evolutionary perspective, men were needed to go out into the world and eliminate outside threats to the family. They had to be on the alert for predators, wild animals, enemies, looters and rival clans. That meant that they were attuned to looking at the horizon, scanning for danger, always ready and alert. That also meant that they have been genetically wired to pay more attention to things outside their homes and families and often miss subtle nuances, cues and disruptions inside the house. They will spot a broken tap or a torn wire more easily than notice a child's mood. Men are genetically disposed to fix, protect, guard and strengthen. That has also made them blind or blinkered to the emotional needs of those around them. A human system can only do so much. For women it worked the other way around from an evolutionary perspective. Having lived more cloistered lives and being eminently able to multitask, read emotional cues or subtle shifts in the needs of those around them and having cared for families for thousands of years, women are better attuned and more adaptable than men.

For a lot of fathers and men in our culture, emotional involvement with their children doesn't come naturally. To be soft and considerate towards their children is to spoil them and also to be seen as a spineless father. In their eyes they are the head of the family, the man who must be heard and obeyed, who has to make sure everyone survives and succeeds. And they end up pushing the same standards of what it means to be successful on their children, often using discipline and force. Again and again some fathers seem compelled to impose themselves like a jealous God on their children, applying unrealistic standards of achievement on boys and strait-jacketing the development of girls, driven only by the conviction that they are always right, free to go or to stay as they choose, seemingly careless of any consequences their attitudes may have on their children. Time and time again, fathers seem to have a gift for the crushing word or gesture whose painful impact remains with the child all its life. How many of us can look back at our own fathers and deny that? Society and the way it functions has kept men away from a powerful truth—that the greatest gift a father can grant his children is to give them permission to claim him as one of their own, to make demands on his heart, not just his purse and to see through him as the vulnerable creature he is inside.

Most children strive to impress their fathers all their lives simply because anything that they do is not enough. Look at your own childhood and many of you will remember the dissatisfaction and disregard of a father at achievements that he considered irrelevant or unimportant. Most children are conditioned to excuse their father's behaviour (often encouraged in this by the mother), blaming his mindlessness on male insensitivities and the rest, on work-related stress. Most children do not recognize the fact that their father's behaviour is who he really is. Most fathers simply forget that a child is not an adult—that they must make allowances and lower their expectations to meet reality. Fathers can learn to grow out of the image of the fearful patriarch and grow into the role of a loving and attentive father who is accessible and amiable. And I think a lot of fathers today are trying to do that by getting in touch with their innate sensitivity denied to them by the unwritten laws of patriarchy. It is very hard work to uncover the softness inside them and it definitely cannot be done unsupported.

Just as women must learn the extent of their power and influence over their children and only opt for motherhood if they can use both gently, so fathers must learn to tread the opposite route. The power of the father is so pervasive that his first step must be to relinquish it. To do this, he can learn to see himself as a responsible adult, not as a competitor to the young newcomer, the foremost of those entitled to lay claim to her (the new mother's) time and love. Today's father can grow down from the stature carved out for him by tradition. He can grow up and out of the excuses that have been his respite for centuries. He can make a conscious choice to be a father, just as his partner too can exercise her right to choose motherhood in all awareness of what it entails. To become a place of comfort, and not fear, for his children, he can try and unlearn the lessons of his own boyhood and stop fighting the tides of change. He can bring himself to willingly accept that there is more to his lifelong task of fatherhood than to just kick a ball around with his children for ten minutes a day or payment of the monthly school fee.

* * *

Eyes wide open

In parenting, as in so many aspects of life, power is the key. Both parents possess enormous power over the little creatures in their care. They also bring to their roles the burden of their own hopes and expectations, fears from their own childhoods that will rear their heads at each milestone their children attempt to cross. Each parent carries his or her own set of misgivings, guilts and biases. As adults who want to be parents and as adults who are parents, it is important to be able to recognize our patterns, recognize our limitations as human beings and as men and women, before we even think of becoming parents.

A child is not a commodity, a blank slate or a pet. It is a sensitive, sentient being in the process of development. Having children, or opting for adoption, as a solution for the loneliness or emptiness that most of us encounter in our lives is simply irresponsible, to say the least. More so now, when older family structures and simpler lives are diminishing, making help and support for new parents more difficult to come by. Parenting should be undertaken with the focus on the chosen child, not to fill a hole in the life of the parents. As with mothering for women, we need to get away from the idea that having a family is an inalienable right and duty for every couple, the only justification for their existence. Teachers, friends, relatives, social-work agencies, adoptive and biological families, ignore this fact at their own peril, and even more so, their children's. We think of children now as a right, not a privilege, not given, but ordered and perfected through genetic modification. We all want families that look well put together—mere props in our increasingly designer lifestyles.

The old template of the family with the hard-working father and homemaker mother with two perfect children is nearly extinct now. Families now come in all shapes, sizes and rearranged combinations. They may be with or without fathers because single women, widows and divorcees choose to parent alone. They may be without mothers too—single parents now include more males as today's divorced or widowed men make the effort to bring up their children by themselves, something almost unheard of before the 1970s. A couple who have only one child may now consider that family, whereas to others it will only feel like a family when it is big enough to play cricket. New family systems call for new challenges and new solutions. But the question remains: how do we build a family today that will be happy in the ordinary, unremarkable way of the past we seem to remember from our own childhoods? How do we create a family of children who know the simple feeling of security and contentment—qualities that defend us best against the violence and destruction that dogs discontentment and insecurity everywhere? Many parents today feel that this is not possible in today's increasingly corrupt world.

In her book, Rosalind Miles confronts us with this resounding question:

What are parents for? There is only one answer—they are for their children.

How do we become what our children need us to be? I do not claim to know all the answers. I am certainly not the perfect parent, struggling as I am financially, psychologically and creatively. And I am fully aware of the mind-bending, heart-expanding lifework that parenting is. My intention here is not to lecture or admonish—we live with too much judgement as it is—but when I see adults sit in my consultation room and break down from all the pain, generational trauma, abuse, name calling and suppression they have faced at the hands of their parents, I know there's something we have been doing wrong.

And with that knowledge we can move ahead, try to be the aware parent, the questioning parent, the parent who attempts to unravel absolute ideas of righteous morality that do more harm than good to our children. And sometimes even that is not enough. Our circumstances, constraints, challenges will push us against the wall, and we will fail many times. We will face joblessness, death, disease, caring for aging parents, heartbreak, divorce, betrayal and anger. We will be cornered by the world and feel limited as humans. There will be days and weeks where we won't be able to show up fully as parents. Our tone will get sharper and spiteful, we will refuse a hug or push away a question. And then we will remember and try again. That's the best we can do, try again and do it with a full sense of both our power and fragility as parents.

To reach deeper awareness about parenting and what it entails, we need to be conscious of the fact that alcohol and drug abuse in children is widespread, child sexual abuse is rampant, anorexia and bulimia in children is common in the world and more parents hurt and violate their children than outsiders do. Without a greater readiness to question the pre-set precepts of parenthood, children like these will keep adding to the numbers we see in newspapers and research papers on childcare and child health. This is why we need to 'unparent' ourselves—to challenge our blind faith in our own parenting competencies and question our unfounded assurance that we are fully equipped and perfect human beings who are eminently capable of taking care of innocent lives. We need to debate this assumed infallibility of our judgement as parents, and seek newer and better ways to deal with the many problems that beset the children of today. We can try to understand parenthood as an election, not an obligation, where each individual takes full responsibility for becoming a parent. We can educate ourselves about the emotional and financial cost of parenting while also educating the young about it.

There will always be those—both men and women—who long for a baby and cherish its life as their most precious achievement. They tenderly raise it to a useful and fulfilled adulthood. Chances are you are one of those parents because you have picked up a book that most would be apprehensive about. Most parents do not even attempt to put into words the feelings that overcame them when they first held the baby who had been longed for. Some women are able to form an almost magical bond with their child from the very moment of its conception. Some fathers intuitively know how to find within themselves the soft place of refuge children need and not be task masters and disciplinarians.

For me, the first sight of my newborn did not stir any such feelings. Instead, I was filled with dread at my sheer incapacity to comprehend what this little bundle of life needed from me. And I couldn't even voice this for fear of being misunderstood or labelled. My connection with my son, my little man was not instant. It has grown over the years because I have worked, and am still working, at it. I have worked at improving my responses to his needs; I have worked at not reacting but understanding; I have worked at unpeeling all those layers of social conditioning, fears, superstitions and misgivings, that are passed on from parent to parent in our culture. And it is an unending labour, exhausting and time consuming. Sometimes I feel I would have done better to just question whether I was ready for a child or not; whether I was even a good fit to be a mother, with a history of attempted suicide and depression. I also wonder whether my son's father would have done better if he had worked on his trauma and grief on losing his mother at a young age. But I didn't know any better, and neither did he. Both of us believed we would be able to do the best we could, that we would instinctively know what was needed. But we failed so many times. I hope you don't.

Deciding, thinking, learning and planning in advance does not mean a betrayal of parental love. Calculating the cost of a child does not mean that we do not know its value. On the contrary, the value that you place on every child only increases when you put consideration for its future above your own romantic fantasies and emotional needs. Perhaps this is where we went wrong, my ex-husband and I. There was a gaping hole in our lives and we believed that our son could fill it. No child can fill a need that has a life of its own, but if given enough thought, consideration and respect, that child can give you a gift of endless love. I humbly and honestly recognize how hard it is to be worthy of such a priceless blessing. This book is merely an attempt, a journey to keep discovering and to keep sharing how to keep earning the pure love that a child has for its parent, especially in moments that challenge us.

Is this asking too much? Under some circumstances it is much too much, a great burden, while under others it is a joy and an enrichment. It all depends on what the parents themselves experienced in the past, and what they have to give.

—Alice Miller, *Banished Knowledge* (1990)

Chapter 1

Body Safety and Abuse Awareness
Kismi toffee bars and the age of innocence

Ammi, teach me how to forget. I want to remember who I
was before I knew blood . . .

When I was six years old, magic was the taste of indulgent
toffee bars melting in my mouth in soft, warm bursts of
caramel. Freedom was the ability to outrun all the boys in my
street and wear my hair really, really short. Strength was the
power in my limbs to climb, jump and break into a sweat only
after everyone else had tired. Beauty was watching my mother
comb her luxuriant hair. And fear, fear was only the thought
of her leaving me alone for another night to be with her
patients at the hospital. But emotions are nebulous, fleeting,
intangible things that you cannot hold on to and the life of
a child will inevitably encounter some reality that will strip
away all magic from a feeling and change it irrevocably.

My weakness for Kismi toffee bars was to become one such reality that changed the way I looked at myself and felt in my body and suddenly the meaning of fear dawned on me. A fifteen-year-old cousin, who was staying with us for a few weeks, took me to the neighbourhood shops every day to buy my favourite toffee bars until I began to trust him completely. Trust him enough to be led into a silent, dark bedroom one hot afternoon while everyone was away—my parents at the hospital, my grandmother asleep and my siblings out and about. Everything I knew about myself changed that afternoon. I learned that my body was not strength but weakness. That it could know more pain than that of exhausted muscles fatigued from running. Since that day, I have not managed to unlearn the taste of molten caramel (now tinged with the iron of blood) or the fear of a hand covering my mouth. Years later, I also learned that I would be wary of anyone who told me I was beautiful.

When Imaad was born a boy, I believed he would be safe from the violation I had experienced as a child, but nothing had prepared me for what I was to learn during the course of my work first as a child-sexual-abuse-prevention-and-awareness trainer and sexuality educator and later as a trauma healer and life coach. Nearly half of the world's sexually abused children are boys and the extent, gravity and nature of abuse has nothing to do with gender, economic class or social status. It was everywhere. It is everywhere. One of the first people to come and speak to me after my first awareness workshop was a man; severely abused in his school's hostel, he battled depression, anxiety and intimacy issues when he got married, and only after years of therapy and support from his wife, became a father to two children.

I did not want to be unprepared or naive like my parents had been. They loved us dearly, but love is not enough.

They had made some unwise choices about the people they trusted and allowed free access in our home even when they weren't present. Although parental presence is no guarantee for preventing abuse, I believe vigilance does play a part in keeping children safe. While the abuse was happening and even afterwards, they weren't aware enough to pick up on the non-verbal signals that something was very wrong in their household. Or maybe there was just too much silence and social censure around discussing issues which weren't very obvious. I believe it still persists despite all our claims of modernity. Some aspects of modern living take longer than usual to modernize, I guess. In the era that they were born and reared in, it was taboo to even hug or kiss one's child openly, let alone teach them to be aware of abuse. It has taken me years to forgive them their limitations. Perhaps the only real test of love is to be able to love despite limitations. I don't know if they have been able to forgive themselves. I can only hope they have.

It is interesting how time and experiences can change the way one interacts with parents over the years. I find myself discussing homosexuality, abuse awareness and sex with my parents quite openly now, something that would have been frowned upon when we were children, simply because to talk of the body was tantamount to being *besharam* (shameless). As if the mere mention of our fears, desires or anxieties was somehow powerful enough to render us naked for the world to see and ridicule. And nudity was sin. Nakedness was considered *haraam* (forbidden). It took me years to let go of that mental veil which reinforced itself with stubborn vehemence each time I undertook a new workshop or engaged in public conversations around sexuality. I've heard this from so many other trainers working in the area of sexuality. How each foray into a new topic is almost like unpeeling our own sense of what is acceptable and what is not, what is permissible and what we consider is out of bounds. Layer by layer, we have found ourselves drawing closer to the truth; that safety and well-being is more important than what is considered proper or modest. The same holds true for parenting. We become better parents when we learn to look beyond what has been taught to us as absolute.

By the time my son was three, I had taught him to identify and name his body parts, including his private parts. My mother would be scandalized at loud demonstrations of everything that looked like a penis to Imaad. A banana was a 'giant penis', a groundnut was a 'dry penis' and every animal within the reach of his chubby hands was examined for the existence or lack of a penis. We were to learn about babies and how they're made through vigorous feline examinations when we brought two kittens home for his ninth birthday. Female cats go into heat every few weeks and like most creatures, our cats copulated openly. Anyone who has been around cats knows that their mating rituals go on for hours, and for days on end. And all this time, Imaad would watch and ask questions. Of course, all of this led to socially awkward situations like the time Imaad decided to ask a shrivelled old aunt of mine if she had a 'tiny pipe-like thing' between her legs like he did. Apparently, he was trying to establish common ground with her because she was a favourite *Naani* (maternal grandma). Needless to say, he was sorely disappointed. In time, he learned that non-penis owners could be friendly too.

I learned to be okay (despite the acute discomfort of my ex-in-laws) with loud pronouncements of 'penis' and 'vagee-ena' in supermarkets and other people's drawing rooms because my embarrassment was less important than my son not knowing which body part could not be touched by anyone else except for washing (with permission) and by a doctor (in the presence of a parent). As he grew older, we established rules about not discussing everything in public and a forewarning when a particularly 'private' query was about to be shot at me. By the time Imaad was six, he had developed a very strong sense of ownership over his body. I had to compromise control over what he chose to wear, or if he wanted to apply lotion or not, because it would be hypocritical of me to be repeatedly saying 'your body belongs to you' all the time and not demonstrating, by my respect of the boundaries, beyond which even I could not venture, that it did indeed belong to him. Forcing him to hug or kiss aunts and uncles whom he didn't feel particularly inclined to hug or kiss, had to go out the window. How could I expect him to recognize and report uncomfortable physical experiences if I forced him to touch, when he didn't want to touch or be touched? I learned to let comments like 'Your son is ill mannered' not bother me. Imaad seeming ill mannered to relatives who forced their unwelcome kisses on him was preferable to his not having the agency to say no to someone crossing his physical boundaries.

However much you may have prepared yourself and however many Safe-and-Unsafe-Touch posters you have gone through with your child, nothing really prepares you for the time your child actually comes over to you and says that something has happened. It is in those moments that your reserves of wisdom, strength and good sense are truly tested. Around the time Imu was seven, our cook, Baji, had begun to bring her twelve-year-old daughter to our house on weekends. Her name was Neelu (name changed). Imaad and she shared a love-hate relationship at the best of times and there were always arguments and fights breaking out with a lot of complaints like 'She coloured on my notebook' and 'She

broke my pen' and so on. It was always difficult to understand
who did what and most of the time I ended up sitting both of
them down to conduct little exercises on sharing.

I found it very hard to be as equitable when my son came to
me one day to tell me that Neelu had asked him to take off his
shorts so she could 'kiss' what was inside. She had also touched
his penis from above his clothes while asking him to lie down
so she could sit on him. Imu said that she thought it would be
fun. All the grown-ups did it. The first emotion I remember
feeling was a blind rage. A primordial fury at someone (even
if it were a child) who had attempted to touch my son in a way
that had made him cry. My little boy was shaken. Despite his
knowing everything I had told him he was afraid and angry. He
wanted me to punish Neelu. A big part of me wanted to punish
her too. But Neelu was twelve. She was a child herself and was
clearly imitating things she had seen. She had no awareness
about boundaries, and she could have seriously traumatized
my son if he'd had no awareness of boundaries either.

In situations like these, it becomes important to look at
the root of the problem while being simultaneously present for
the child who has been frightened and hurt. Some people may
argue that I was under no obligation to understand Neelu's
behaviour and where she was coming from. I should have
just handed her over to Baji (who would have undoubtedly
thrashed her black and blue) and asked Neelu to leave. But I
felt that it *was* my duty to speak to her just as it was my job to
reassure my son that he was safe and to let him know that he
had been very brave to tell me everything. In my experience
as a Child Sexual Abuse (CSA) trainer, I have learnt that many
young adults and adolescents end up hurting younger children
because they have no awareness of their growing sexuality
or respecting other people's bodily privacy. And one cannot

argue that this happens only in lower-income-group families. It happens in wealthy families too. There is no conversation around bodily curiosity in most families. While some may tell their children to report unsafe touch, they may skip telling them how not to touch someone else.

Because Imu was very upset, I did ask Neelu not to come to our house but only after I had explained to her that it was not okay to touch anyone else inappropriately or to copy adult behaviour thoughtlessly. From then on, I kept an eye on Neelu and always ensured that I spoke to her without hostility or rancour whenever I met her. I also had to speak to her mother about being careful around growing children, to talk to them openly and to tell them what was okay for them to do and what wasn't. But what do you tell someone who lives in a single room with her husband and three growing children? You just hope that they have the good sense to be discreet in some things and more forthcoming in others. What happened in my house, while I was in the vicinity, is not what most childhood sexual abuse looks like. In most cases, crossing a child's physical boundaries is more covert, often violent and accompanied by threats and coercion especially if the offender is an adult. This was nowhere near that, but it was still enough to terrify a young child.

When it comes to body safety and abuse awareness, most parents baulk at the thought of describing that kind of violence to innocent children. It doesn't have to be this way. Teaching body safety does not mean controlling our children or limiting the way they interact with people by using fear as a tool to keep them safe. That will only diminish their sense of trust in the world around them. Strong terms like 'good and bad' touch can further limit the way children perceive touch and take away the natural warmth that this essential human connection can impart to any interaction. I prefer using terms like 'safe and unsafe' where safe touches are loving and respectful but are also described as touches that may feel unpleasant sometimes—like a dentist treating a cavity, or a strong grasp while crossing the road—but are essential for a child's safety. And unsafe touches are described as touches that can cause hurt or harm—like touching a hot iron, picking up broken glass *and* anyone touching a child's private parts or body in a way that hurts or causes discomfort, especially if that touch is accompanied by threats and bribes.

To be a parent is to learn to love unconditionally, despite everything that pushes us to not be kind or tender; it is to learn to control our anger and ignore our frustration. To be a parent is also to learn to accept fear as a natural companion to that love—fear for your child's safety, fear that the horrors of the world will constrict your child's freedom and joy. Here's a small list of things that can help you navigate that fear better. They have helped me.

Naming private parts

From the time your children learn to speak and identify body parts, include teaching them how to name their body parts properly. Using names like wee-wee and shame-shame or chi-chi, somehow transfers the idea that private parts are a thing of shame. We do need to teach our children to talk about their bodies, to be mindful of their own and other people's boundaries; however, doing so in a way that induces shame and a sense that our bodies are places of secrecy, is not healthy.

What you can say is things like, 'Your body belongs to you and the parts that are under your bathing suit are your personal, private body parts that no one else should touch.

Only mummy and daddy can change or shower you and even then, we need to ask. Or a doctor can see you if it's needed but never alone.'

Creating a sense of normalcy around our bodies goes a long way in helping children build confidence about how they look and feel while also making it easy to talk about anyone touching them.

Also tell your kids that it's not okay for anyone to show them their personal parts or show them nude pictures and videos. Sharing pornography or asking children to watch as the offender undresses or bathes are some of the methods that serial abusers use to make their victims feel like it's okay to do this, to make them feel included in the process. This makes it difficult for children to report abuse later because they are made to feel that they were complicit co-conspirators in the deed and therefore they could be dubbed as guilty. Especially if it's someone known to the child and there is established trust or friendship. So, if a child knows that a penis is a penis and a vulva is a vulva, he or she will know what to say to you if someone touches them or flashes them. You could talk about body parts while bathing a child, while labelling body parts on a chart or while reading a board book about bodies. You don't have to do this every day, just often enough to be remembered.

Teaching kids to recognize the early warning signs

Children are very strongly intuitive. They are often the first to notice missing things, people and changes in routine. As much as they rebel against their daily routines, they need those routines and boundaries to feel safe. A predictable pattern makes children comfortable and it is for this reason that they'll intuitively know if something is amiss. Nature has strongly wired us to sense fear and discomfort and our bodies respond to these very clearly. Our hands get clammy, we feel like throwing up or we start sweating. Our job is simply to make children aware of these natural warning signs that manifest in any difficult situation so that they know that something is amiss and are able to report it *even* if it doesn't feel like that at first.

For example, if a known person in a position of trust and power begins to inappropriately touch a child, the child may not feel that something is amiss in the beginning since there's a sense of connection in place. But as soon as there's a shift in the adult's breathing or touching, the child's body will react with discomfort. If we're able to teach our children to not ignore this discomfort, even if it's someone whom the child respects or fears, and teach the child to try to shout, move away or call for help as soon as they feel threatened (in the presence of anyone), we'll actually be able to prevent serious damage in most situations.

To make things simple, use words like, 'When you feel your tummy cramping, or when you feel icky and sweaty, or your heart beats too fast, your body is sending a message—it is saying go and get help! You have to listen to your body when that happens.'

Of course, this is for children who are a little older; but in my experience, it works with kids as young as three and four as well. Throw in some words like vomit and poop and you're sure to have their attention!

Creating a safety net of trusted adults

Much as we may wish that our children always come to us for help or that we're always present when they happen to need us, it's not always going to be possible. Sometimes, our children may not want to talk to us, especially in the case of older kids; sometimes they may be away at school or camp when they need to talk about difficult things. And it's up to us to make sure that our children know who they can go to in a crisis or when they want to share something. To make this possible, sit with your kids and ask them to name five trusted adults who they feel safe and comfortable with. Please resist the urge to suggest names and please don't feel disappointed if you don't make the list, although that will hurt. Point out that the names could be of anybody from home, school or neighbourhood and extended family. Someone they can go to or call. Next, make your children write down the names of these five adults on a sheet of paper that says my trusted people or something similar. For younger children, you could use pictures and names to make it easier for them to remember.

Once the sheet is ready, playfully talk about why your kids feel safe around those whose names are on it, possibly write what they say on the sheet. This is just to make sure these adults are loved not just because they bring gifts or treats but because they induce a certain feeling in the children who adore them. Maybe Mala Aunty is special because she is kind, Sameer Chacha is a favourite because he's funny and Amita Ma'am is nice because she doesn't say things like 'you're stupid'. Feeling association is important for children and to be reminded of that makes that association stronger. The people on the list will also need to be told that they have earned a place of privilege in your child's life and that they need to be ready if they are ever needed. Put that sheet up on your fridge or somewhere prominent so that it's a constant visual reminder for all of you without being intimidating.

Learning to say no

So much of what we learn about parenting is to do with creating obedient offspring, perfect children who move, speak and behave the way we want them to. That is how we were brought up and it's hard to look beyond our conditioning and see that older methods of parenting robbed children of their voices in many ways. Yes, it's important to teach children to listen to what is good for them, like eating healthy food and studying well. But that discipline need not extend to controlling their sense of comfort, their sense of self and the strong wills that children are born with. Teaching them to *always* obey, to always say yes, even if they're not happy about something, is in a way teaching them that they should abandon how they feel in favour of gaining social approval.

Will a child who has been taught to put up with bad behaviour by a sibling or a friend know how to walk out of a toxic relationship when he's older? Will a child who is forced to touch, hug or go to people he does not like going to, be able to report abuse if his physical boundaries are violated? Will a child who has been taught to believe that saying yes to everything is the only way to earn love ever be able to say no? The answer to all these questions is perhaps, no.

We need to teach our children to say no if something makes them very unhappy. And before we can do that, we need to learn to say no ourselves. That party you should go to, but don't want to because you don't like being around those present, means that you should just politely decline. That friend who rubs you the wrong way and makes you feel small, tell her it's best if you don't meet. Say no to things and people that don't give you the joy they're supposed to. Gently, politely, but firmly, say no. Say no so your children can see that it is okay to say no to things that hurt us or cause us discomfort.

This is not merely a question of your children saying no to unwanted touch, but also about developing their ability to extricate themselves from potentially damaging relationships and situations that they may feel obliged to stay in just because they haven't been taught to value their own needs. For younger children, using simple and familiar words that they can use and need to remember, like 'No', 'Stop', 'Run', 'Scream', in case someone touches their genitals or comes too close for comfort, will work. Write them down on a sheet of paper under a simple heading like My Body Safety Rules along with things like 'No Secrets. Tell mummy if someone makes you uncomfortable and safe touches are okay but unsafe touches are not okay'. Pin the sheet where everyone can see it and you just have to gently remind kids to remember these rules if they're going for a party, picnic or sleepover.

Teaching body safety doesn't mean constricting movement or creating fear about strangers and touches. It is all about awareness of what is okay and what is not okay. Some of our most enriching experiences are based on interactions with people we have never met before, or warm exchanges that have come out of the blue. So, saying things like 'never hug, smile at or talk to strangers' can create a sense of otherness and fear about the world in general. It's okay to show physical affection *if* your children feel safe and want to engage like that. And when they know that they have the right to negotiate (a) what they like and what they don't like and (b) what is safe and what is not, they will be empowered enough to say no and ask for help if they need it. Trust in that.

Saying no to secrets

Children love secrets, they get excited about secrets, but some secrets can be very harmful. When you begin talking about body safety with your children, teach them to differentiate between secrets and surprises. Surprises, like a birthday party or a gift or a trip, are okay because they are eventually disclosed and also because they are joyful. Secrets are meant to be hidden and anything that needs to be kept hidden from parents could be unsafe. Creating secrets around touching is often a ploy used by serial abusers to involve children in a 'game' and that sense of secrecy can prevent a child from reporting abuse later. So, anything that someone asks to keep a secret should be a no-go zone for your children.

Gently remind your children that you will never be angry at them for talking about anything that a friend or an adult asked to keep secret. That the things people don't want their parents to know are often unsafe and dangerous. So, while surprises are happy and welcome, secrets are not welcome or allowed.

Paying attention to unusual behaviour

It's so easy to get swept up in our daily routines and miss out on warning signs that something is not right with our children. And sometimes, we're aware of this nagging feeling in the back of our minds that there's something going on but we still miss talking about it, exploring it. Maybe because we're terrified of what we'll find out if we dig deeper. Confronting our anxiety and fears is better than a lifetime of guilt. Or so my parents tell me.

If you observe any uncharacteristic changes in your child's behaviour like fits of anger, or low-level anxiety, inability to focus, difficulty sleeping, bed wetting, fear of going out or reacting anxiously in the presence of someone in particular, please ask your child what is bothering them.

Be gentle, be patient and above all, keep telling them that no matter what happens they will be loved and protected. Of course, some changes can be explained by growth phases or other stresses but it's helpful to rule out abuse so that it can be prevented from happening again and your child can get the help they need.

In very young children and toddlers, redness or swelling around the genitals, crying and screaming every time diapers are changed, refusing to leave you, or refusing to go to a particular person, can all be signs of abuse. It's important to pay attention to who cares for your children in your absences, who is allowed access to your house, and if your older children are clear about who is allowed into their bedrooms and who is not. I understand that all of this may seem frightening and it's easy to slip into being helicopter parents who are always on their toes. But these are only guidelines and if you have these in place and are able to gently, non-threateningly remind your children about their body safety rules, you should be okay.

Responding with attention and care

Despite all our awareness and homework, when it comes to an actual incident that has affected our children, our hearts simply cave and we may not remember to respond the way our children need us to respond. Our own fears, anguish and pain comes centre stage and we forget, we simply forget, that our focus *must* only be on the child who has been hurt. Everything else can come later.

If your child ever tells you that someone hurt them sexually, believe them. Children don't make up stories like that. They are wary of upsetting family situations and if they name someone they have known and trusted, please understand that the child has already suffered in the process of coming to you because he has pushed aside his fear and shame. Tell them you believe them and that you will do everything in your power to keep them safe. But do remember to not promise more than you can actually do. In situations where the abuser is a family member, it is difficult to keep abusers away although that is exactly what you should do.

Make sure your child is physically taken care of and that you contact a medical professional if you think that necessary. Every family's circumstances will determine the course of action they take in terms of legal issues, but what your child needs from you is to be believed and to be heard. Don't ask leading questions. Let the child find their comfort in telling you; simply be present, listen and keep telling them—'it's not your fault'. No matter what the circumstances, abuse is *never* a child's fault. Our responses in the event of abuse can make or break a child's recovery. The child should never know about your struggle to address the issue or hear from you what you had to do later. It's not her fault just as it wasn't yours. All that matters is that your child feels safe now.

Practise active listening

I often say this in my workshops, 'Our relationship with our children is their best means of protection,' and I mean it. In the decade since I have had Imaad teach me, test me and love me like no one else had done before, I have become absolutely sure of one thing—as long as I listen to his crazy alien stories, awful poop jokes and anxious questions about bullying, with attention, patience and love, he will tell me everything. Just as he told me that Neelu tried to touch him or that he doesn't like the neighbourhood watchman teasing him, or that a boy in class kissed a girl on the lips. If I listen to the small stuff with presence and without judgement, I trust he will tell me the big stuff too.

I ask you to trust in that too.

Chapter 2

Bodily Curiosity and Discovery

'Amma, why do women have these soft, round thingies
and men don't? I think it's very unfair.'
'Amma, do penises die in the mornings and get rigor
mortis? Mine acts strange every morning when I wake up.
Then it comes back to life again.'
'Amma, why do we need to wear clothes? I hate clothes in
the summer.'
'Amma!! Baby is pulling his wee-wee so hard it will fall
off!! Come quickly and have a look!'

Imagine being bushwhacked by any of these questions and
statements five days out of ten. Now imagine trying not to
react or yell or laugh as you attempt to pause and respond
with just the right amount of information. A bit of an ask
even for the most sensitized parent I would say! The above
exclamations and questions are from my own life—the crazy,

funny, sometimes lonely, life I shared with my eleven-year-old son. I've have learned to fill my life with little pauses to make room for all the wonder this child brings into my life—sometimes gently and at other times with a bang! These pauses can make all the difference between an angry rebuff and a warm, honest answer to a curious child's question as he learns to make sense of everything around him.

Adults often wonder why bodies are so important for little ones, why a child's first response to any human being entering his field of vision is touch. Tiny pink, squiggly fingers searching for noses, reaching out to pull at moustaches, exploring and getting lost in a forest of beards, tugging at loose tresses—these are some very common experiences that we've encountered while holding or touching a baby for the first time. I remember my child establishing the identity of his father by touching his moustache each time he visited from the far-flung country where he had been stationed for work. In the first few months, he would look at his dad's bushy face and bury his own in my neck. This face was not familiar, it wasn't the smooth face of his mother or the bald face of his grandfather. Little by little he would be coaxed into his father's waiting arms and his first point of contact would be the moustache. By the time he was eight months old, any man with a moustache was 'Abba (dad)', which was, naturally, a tad uncomfortable for me; but for him, it was the physical roadmap to his father's being.

Babies enter the world without a map, without any 'How To' manuals and their sole reference point, to begin with, is their own body. The desire to touch, feel, taste and grab at things in their line of vision are literally the first steps they take in this world. Curiosity manifesting as touch is the foundation of their first interactions with their surroundings. With eyes that can barely focus before twelve weeks of age, their hands become their eyes. Babies are little seekers, eager to explore, eager to learn, eager to sense everything around them—they are little sponges that absorb with each pore and every cell in their bodies.

And yet we find ourselves surprised when little boys and girls spend hours picking at their noses, trying to assess the dimensions of these curious little holes in the middle of their faces. We find ourselves reacting negatively when we see a little boy pull out his penis during a bath and examine it with all the seriousness of a zoologist inspecting a new species of bird or insect.

'Bad manners!' we imperiously declare. But give me one man or woman who has never explored their nose or fumbled around in their knickers and shorts as kids and I will shave off my eyebrows, I promise! For children, what is there not to see? What is there not to discover and explore? Little folds that expand and contract on their own! Oooh. Mysterious dark caves that hold wonder upon wonder of little boogers— in different colours, textures (and tastes!). Strange sensations that feel pleasurable and therefore they need to be felt again and again. But why does Mummy say that makes me a bad boy? I'm only exploring!

I remember when Imaad was barely four years old, we were extremely busy in our daily business of serious 'pottification'. Sitting on the toilet seat was as serious as preparing for a meeting. We needed books to keep the little one distracted, we needed a mother to be present and ready, answering all sorts of questions that arose in the little one's mind while he strained and forgot to strain. And we needed entertainment, offering a little toy or a little ball that could be squished and pulled apart so that the toddler would stay on the pot long enough to finish his business.

On this particularly busy day, as I bent down to help my young man wash himself after a big dump, I found him peering rather curiously into my T-shirt which was hanging low at the neck.

'Amma what is that? What are those big, round, squishy things?' Now I know I have always been a big woman, something that has been the source of much embarrassment and unwanted attention most of my life, but nothing really prepared me for such a direct scrutiny by my own offspring! It took me all of two seconds to regain my composure and remind myself that this was a child—a curious, affable child who only wanted to know.

'Well, these are called breasts,' I stated simply as I straightened up. Of course, a simple statement would never suffice to satiate the curiosity of a four-year-old and what followed was a very detailed examination of the 'two spongy bits' as my little man decided to call them. The conversation went somewhat like this:

I: 'But why do you have them, Amma?'

A: 'I have them because all women have them.'

I: 'But why do all women have them?'

A: 'Imu, all women have them because they need them when they have babies. You see, we use breasts to feed our babies, like how I used to feed you with a little bottle when you were a baby?'

I: 'But why?'

A: 'Because when babies are born, our bodies generate milk so that we may be able to feed our babies and keep them healthy. It is something all mamas do, even animal mamas. You know, like cows, like goats, even cats. It's like . . . I give you food now, but when you were a baby and didn't have teeth, I gave you milk from my own body.'

I: 'Oh, okay. So these are like snacks for babies?'

A: (Flinching.) 'Not snacks, but food, yes, or where food comes from. Mamas bodies make the best food for babies. Babies have no teeth to chew with and mama's milk keeps the baby healthy.' (I was hoping we'd stop with this, before something else came up . . . but luck has never been on my side.)

I: 'But tell me one thing, Amma, why do men not have these thingies?'

A: 'Not "THINGIES", Imaad. Breasts, we call them breasts.'

I: 'Okay, okay, breasts. Why do men not have breasts? Why does Nanu have no breasts? I have seen him in a towel, he doesn't have anything like this. He's all *ganjoo* (literally means bald but I think Imu meant smooth) there. Even Abba doesn't have anything like this. I think that's very unfair. You talk about boys and girls being equal, but girls have something that boys don't,' said my little one with an expression that bordered on disgust and deep disappointment (this is what you get when you try and raise a baby who is aware of gender equality before he even begins school!).

A: 'I understand that this feels unfair, Imu, but Nature decided that only women will have the ability to feed their babies from their bodies and men would do other things to look after their babies. Like bringing them food when they were older, helping them climb a tree or sometimes even bathe them when a mum was busy doing other things. You see, babies need a lot of care and if both mummy and daddy had these, they would both have to feed their babies. Then who would do the rest of the work?' There was a pause and I dared to breathe and get up. But it wasn't meant to be. Sigh.

I: 'But why do only older women have breasts? Why does Alina not have them, why do none of my classmates have them? They are girls too!' Alina was Imaad's playmate and neighbour and they were very competitive.

This was getting out of hand, I muttered to myself. This was too much! I was going to have to explain puberty and menstruation and changes in bodily functions to him when he was four and I wasn't ready! I was flustered and impatient. I knew that I was supposed to answer all these questions calmly and accurately, but I also understood that giving him too much information all at once would probably confuse him. So, I chose a short, crisp sentence that would probably answer his question but also stop him from asking those whose answers he wasn't ready for. I took a deep breath and went for it, very serious and calm.

A: 'You see, Imaad, as we grow older a lot of changes happen in the bodies of both boys and girls. When girls grow older, they develop breasts, just like when boys grow older, they develop moustaches and beards. You know, like Faizi *maamu* (uncle) had a smooth face when he was younger, but he has a *daadhi* (beard) now. That way. Does that answer your question? Because I think we've been in the toilet for far too long and it's getting very smelly and hot. We really do need to get out.'

I: 'Okay, Amma, I get it. But I still don't get one thing— why would Nature give boys only these little round brown things and not the whole thing?' Imu pointed at his nipples with a genuinely confused expression. 'What's the point of giving boys something, if it can't do anything, you know?'

Now I hope to God your little one is not given to asking questions that would leave a so-called expert like me wondering, but in my case, Imaad's curiosity is the fodder for many funny posts on my Facebook. But I wasn't prepared for this.

A: 'Well you know, Imu, Nature hasn't given everything to everyone. That way everyone has something unique and different. So, girls get breasts that feed babies and boys have nipples, so they don't feel left out!'

I: 'Like consolation prizes? That's nice, Amma. Now I don't feel bad. At least these are decorative,' he smiled and ran off stroking his poky little chest.

I remember feeling unsettled after this exchange. In hindsight, my response feels very crass and not informative but this goes to show that even when you think you're prepared, children ask questions that leave you stumped. If Imaad had asked me this when he was thirteen or fourteen, I could have told him how nipples in males are a source of play and pleasure. But at that moment, I just didn't know what else to say. When I think about it now, I feel that a more appropriate response could have been something like this:

'Have you noticed how all trees have green leaves and colourful flowers? If you look at the trunk, you'll notice that the bark on trees is brown in colour. They look the same, but there are some things that are different. You know that tree in front of our gate, it has orange flowers and its trunk is thin and long. And that big tree in your school playground, the one with the swing underneath? It has yellow flowers and a huge, thick trunk. Trees do look the same but there are small differences. In the same way, human beings look the same. We have arms, legs, eyes, hands. But if you look closely, there will be differences. Our faces look different, men have flat chests and women have breasts. Beings in nature are similar but also unique in their own ways. Men and women can look similar if they wear the same kind of clothes, but our bodies are different.'

When you read this conversation here, it seems like it happened over a span of fifteen to twenty minutes, but the truth is, this conversation was barely two or three minutes long. Toddlers aren't really patient people. And in those two or three minutes, I had to come up with a pat answer that reflected no shame or discomfort while also being age appropriate and honest. As I mentioned before, children are highly intuitive. With their invisible antennae, they pick up easily on the non-verbal cues we emit through our body language and the way we say things. But I realize that our culture hasn't really been the most supportive when it comes to talking about our bodies, especially parts that are 'supposed' to be sexual like breasts, vulvas and penises. But the thing with children is, the more you try to hide something, or try to create a sense of mysterious censure around topics, the more their curiosity will grow; because children are curious little detectives, hard-wired to learn and ask. That is how they function. They understand the world through their eyes, their other senses and whatever strikes them as odd, different or simply new, will spike their curiosity.

If you're not going to tell them things they want to know, chances are they'll cook up ridiculous stories themselves with the help of the junior grapevine association. We might as well prepare ourselves in advance. We are the first people they're going to come to with their catechism—questions which might sometimes seem funny and sometimes downright uncomfortable. We feel uncomfortable because we haven't been taught to regard these questions as natural. For most of us, asking questions was simply out of the question. We were supposed to accept things, without question, the way they were handed down to us; information was standard, much like two plus two equals four. Too much questioning was tantamount to a form of disobedience—a sign of rebellion and misbehaviour. Perhaps that is why so many of us still feel ashamed and guilty when it comes to topics about our bodies, sexuality and even sex.

There are people I've met over the course of my work who have asked me whether it is necessary to include sexuality education (larger umbrella term of sexuality education that includes sex ed, body safety and info on sexual orientation, gender and relationships) in the school curriculum. They wonder whether it would be more appropriate to talk about sexuality and sex when the kids were older; for example, when they were seventeen or eighteen? I tell them that sexuality education is not merely about reproduction, intimacy or abuse awareness. Sexuality education should begin right after birth because sexuality begins immediately after birth. Teaching kids about their bodies should ideally begin when children are young and should not be waitlisted to a lecture given at puberty. Sexuality is this vast umbrella of topics that includes bodily curiosity, abuse awareness, basic knowledge about gender and sex education as well as thoughts, feelings, consent and relationships. It's not something you can thrust without any warning on teenagers and expect them to understand things they have never been familiar with up until then.

I remember the first time I entered a swimming pool; the water engulfed everything—both my body and my mind. I was only aware of how it moved and shifted around me, not so much about my body. When I stepped out of the pool, it felt like I was experiencing my limbs and skin for the first time. I remember thinking that this was probably how babies felt when they emerged from their mother's womb. As they grow, their bodies are the first milestones on their journey of discovering the world. This curiosity to discover grows if they're around older children and have lots of opportunities to observe how different everybody is.

Last year, my little nephew was visiting us, and it was our job to bathe him every night before bed. The little monkey made it a habit to play with his penis in the tub every day. Imaad, who was watching him one day, shrieked in alarm when Baby pulled at his penis so hard that it looked like it would detach and come loose in his hand!

'*Ukkhad jaegi!*' (It will come off) is the Urdu phrase I remember Imu screaming in panic. I thought it was uniquely hilarious, but I didn't dare show it. Despite the screaming and protesting from the baby when I gently tried to extract his suffering member from his pincer grip, this spectacle offered a perfect opportunity to explain to both the boys that penises are delicate things and must be handled with care. Little Nanhu continued to protest and scream until he was taken out of the tub, but Imaad understood. I also thought it was a good time to tell Imaad that touching oneself was a natural, pleasurable activity and nothing to be afraid about or ashamed of. Perhaps that is why his little brother was enjoying it so much. One must be gentle and make sure there's no one around. Since Nanhu was a baby, he didn't understand that, but he would learn as he grew older.

It makes me very sad to see that so many of us are brought up with a sense of extreme shame about our bodies. We spend much of our pre-teen years trying to hide ourselves from the public gaze. I remember being constantly reminded to cover my bosom with a *dupatta* (a long scarf) and being told to wear long-sleeved kurtas and dresses. It wasn't very comfortable, especially in the sweltering heat of Indian summers, but that is how we were brought up in a semi-conservative Muslim household. I don't blame my parents. I understand that they are a product of their time and that they were merely echoing patterns and etiquettes that had been drummed into them when they were children themselves.

I am not saying that dressing modestly is bad or that covering yourself is not modern. Personal style of clothing should be a choice and not forced. Children who are brought up being shamed into covering themselves or being ostracized for asking questions about their bodies often grow up with a sense of shame. This later affects their self-worth and creates body image issues, which are psychologically damaging. Bodies are beautiful, they house our spirit, our very being. In all cultures, bodies have been described as the temple of life. How can it be shameful to explore this beautiful building in which our spirit resides? Exploring and getting to know our bodies is as natural as breathing. Nobody teaches babies to touch themselves or to play endlessly with their fingers, their arms and their tiny feet. They do it because it comes naturally to them. Everything about their bodies, everything about the bodies of the people around them is a source of wonder to them.

And it is indeed wondrous! This beautiful, varied, differently coloured, human machine manifests itself so uniquely in different parts of our planet. White, brown, black—so many colours, so many physical attributes—it is a thing of incessant wonder, exploration and gratitude. This is what we need to pass on to our children if we are to allow them freedom of expression and exploration and the space to learn things about their own selves. It is never easy, given that we are conditioned by our upbringing. It determines a lot of the ways we parent and respond intuitively. Let me share a few ways which may make this process a little easier for all of us.

Bodily curiosity is natural—Rinse and repeat

Whenever your child, or any child around you for that matter, exhibits signs of curiosity about their body or somebody else's, take a deep breath and tell yourself that this is completely natural. Your first impulse will be to stop them from doing whatever it is that he or she is doing and reprimand the child because that is the way we've been brought up. I urge you to pause and take a step back. Examining our own notions of morality, of what is natural or unnatural will help us separate our conditioned response from the need of the moment. It will give us a sense of responding with empathy to every situation that we've been put in. If we react with anger or alarm, we're only making sure that a child never feels comfortable about asking us questions about his or her body or sharing anything that he sees or hears.

For example, if a child is watching his younger sister being changed and is observing the difference between his and her private parts, it is likely that he will ask you a question about why her body is different from his. Instead of shushing your boy and saying that it is improper to ask questions like these and that he mustn't ever point out his sister's body, you could use this moment as a 'teaching window'. You could gently go on to tell him about the differences in the bodies of boys and girls and how it is completely natural. If you are someone who believes in gender inclusivity and diversity, you can also use this moment to explain to your child how there are many different types of bodies and that the private parts of these bodies may look different from those of either boys or girls. Some bodies may even have the private parts of both a boy and a girl and that is also completely natural. By explaining these differences with empathy and compassion you're also inculcating acceptance as a value in your child. He will understand diversity as natural while growing up and will remember to treat those who look and behave differently with respect and empathy.

Understanding the difference between curiosity and sexual activity

We all remember that moment in time when we first encountered pleasurable sensations in our nether regions. You might have been taught to deceive yourself into thinking that such moments never existed but if you try and go back to your childhood, I am sure you would remember the first time you discovered bodily pleasure. It isn't necessary that this occurred during your teen years or later. It is completely possible that you experienced this pleasurable surprise when you were barely a child of seven or younger. It is very common for children to explore their genitalia and find it very pleasurable. Male and female genitalia consist of thousands of nerve endings and any sort of physical stimulation is extremely appealing. It makes us feel good. This does not mean that when children come across this peculiar sensation, they are aware of the sexual connotations of pleasure. For children, exploring their genitalia and pleasure is separate from sexual feeling simply because they are not aware of sexual intimacy with another human being in the same way that preteens, teenagers and adults are.

For a little boy, touching his penis is simply as pleasurable as perhaps eating an ice cream, or sliding his nose across a cold windowpane. It's an unusual feeling, it's new and therefore he explores it more. For a little girl, exploring her clitoris (yes, say it, clitoris) for the first time is just as surprisingly joyful as experiencing different flavours and textures of various kinds of ice cream in her mouth. As she swirls the ice cream in her mouth, she discovers the bumpiness of nuts and the saltiness of caramel; each new texture creating a little 'pop' in her mind. How is that bad? Do you remember the first time you touched yourself? What came first, the pleasure of discovering a new sensation or the feeling that this was 'wrong'? My guess is the former came first followed by what you had heard about children touching themselves. Self-exploration does not make children 'immoral' or hypersexual. And yet, it is very common for parents to reprimand and severely punish their small children for exploring their genitals in public or even stripping in public. Such activities may seem alarming to the people around, but in no way does it warrant such an extreme reaction from adults. All we need to do when this happens is gently take the child's hand away from wherever it is and distract him if he or she is very young. Our sense of bodily exposure is loaded with socialized norms around what is appropriate or not. Children don't have any of that. For them, self-exploration is just that—discovery.

If you have an older child who touches himself in public, when you take the child back home, take the time to explain to him that touching oneself, although natural, is a private activity and should be indulged in when no one is around. That way you make sure that you're not offending anybody if a child touches themself in public while also creating a sense of normalcy around physical exploration for your child. Screaming, shouting or any other harsh reaction upon observing a child's innocently exploring touch can lead to feelings of severe guilt, shame and discomfort around sex, pleasure and intimacy when a child grows to be an adult. In some cases, it may also become a deterrent to a healthy and fulfilling sexual life.

There are instances when a habit is developed, and it becomes difficult to keep explaining things gently with no effect. In such cases, it is sensible to consult a doctor or a counsellor and rule out infection, itching and abuse. It is also wise to remember that children today are bombarded with sexualized images from all forms of media. There may be instances when they're simply re-enacting something they have seen. In that case, you need to set proper context and boundaries to avoid misinformation. We'll discuss this at length in later chapters.

Not too much and not too little

Right then, we know how not to react emotionally or irrationally to something that a child is saying or doing out of mere curiosity. We are prepared with the right kind of words and the right attitude. We know that we are aware, introspective parents. We do not want to burden our children with the conditioned responses that we grew up with. But do we know everything? I don't think anyone can say that, least of all me. Parenting is a very curious journey that involves not just learning from the outside but also unlearning from the inside. One of the ways to do this is to intuitively think of the time when you were of the age that your child is. Think about what your favourite activities used to be, how you used to think and feel. Chances are that it would be very hard to recall the exact feelings or sensations that you went through but even if you get a little close, it might help in learning to empathize with what your child needs and how much of it is okay for him or her.

In our nervousness and apprehension while dealing with awkward situations, it is common to give too much information or ask leading questions when it should be the child who sets the standard for how much he or she wants to know or already knows. The danger in giving too much information is that a child might get more confused than they initially were. As it is, we are often afraid that describing something physical or giving information related to sexuality can induce kids to experiment. But I feel that our fear has more to do with how we feel about sexuality rather than what our kids may or may not do. That said, giving away too much information before a child is ready can add to your misgivings. The key is to keep our answers very simple and short and as honest as is age appropriate for the child.

For example, while talking about breasts with my four-year-old son I did not even hint at their sexual aspect to our anatomy. I did not tell him that nipples in both males and females can be a source of playfulness and play a part in lovemaking. I could not tell him this because he simply wasn't ready for this kind of information. There was no language with which I could describe all of this without confusing him and bombarding him with things that he didn't need to know/ wasn't ready to know. If a similar conversation had happened with a thirteen or fifteen-year-old, I would have tweaked it accordingly and included the aspect of sexual pleasure both in the context of sex and masturbation (yes, yes, no avoiding that, please!).

Similarly, in the beginning of the chapter there is an exclamation which describes Imaad asking questions about why his penis is stiff in the morning when he wakes up. I remember this happened when he was six. I told him that that had happened because he had spent an entire night without being to the loo and that the stiffening of his penis was a sign that his body needed to go to the bathroom. Now if he had been fifteen (although I am sure he'd know more about hard-ons by then!) I would have also included the biology behind erections.

Conversely, if we say too little and answer in monosyllables or cryptic remarks, we convey the wrong message that the voices of our children are not important to us. We insinuate that whatever they are struggling to understand can be dismissed as trivial and unworthy of discussion. There is nothing sadder for a child than to feel unheard and not be considered important enough to be valued with presence. The emotional and physical space that we give our children and the value that we place on their words and actions goes on to determine their sense of self later in life. Saying too little or being abrupt may inadvertently encourage unnecessary curiosity in the topic that is being discussed. The child may feel that you are shying away from describing something that is secretive and as we all know, secrets are to children what honey is to bees.

Sex education and schools

In an ideal world, sex education at home is best accompanied with sex education at school, schools being places where kids spend a major chunk of their time every day. When sex education is available both at home and at school, children get similar messages around sexuality and their bodies. Ideally, it makes for a more wholesome approach towards understanding the subject. But that cannot be guaranteed really. A lot of schools use approaches like 'good and bad touch' to teach body safety and as discussed in the earlier chapter, that can be misleading for children. A lot of schools completely opt out of including sex education in their curriculum. The stand a school may take and how inclusively and openly it teaches sex education depends a lot on the ethos of each school. Sex education is a mandatory part of school curriculum in government schools, but private schools may or may not include it.

The best you can do in these circumstances is request your child's school to include sex education, offer information and support about facilitators and resources, or offer to be a learning/teaching partner with the school. I have tried all of the above, but it didn't work with my child's school. They were just not open to the idea. And I realized it's something I should have paid attention to when I was looking for schools. In Imaad's school, sex education is limited to teaching 'The Reproductive System' in biology class in class eight. There's nothing beyond that. But a lot of schools today are making an effort to be more broadminded in their approach with workshops on body safety, puberty and sexuality.

If your child's school does have sex education, please make sure to go through any material the school provides and to regularly chat with your child about what teachers share. Pay special attention to any words that indicate a moral sense like good, bad or dirty. You can reframe these with more generic terms. Sex education is only as effective, diverse and inclusive as the person or people teaching it. And teachers, just like us, come from their own cultural and social contexts. And all of us need to put in work in unlearning socialized messages. If sex education in school reflects a purity culture where abstinence is advocated through the language of sin, heaven or hell, you're in trouble. Sex education is not about religious doctrines but about understanding facts about our bodies and relationships from a perspective of health.

For parents who have had no exposure to sex education, schools teaching it can come as a shock. I remember when my school conducted seminars on sexuality when I was in grade eleven. It must've been 1999. The school had called in experts from Delhi and handed out lovely books by TARSHI (Talking about Reproductive and Sexual Health Issues). I still have my copy of The Blue Book, which was distributed to older kids. When I look back, I do feel that my school did a good job at providing information. The atmosphere was safe and even teachers left the students with the trainers to allow for more freedom to ask questions. But I also remember that there was a huge backlash from a lot of parents. They accused the school of corrupting the kids and teaching them how to have sex. Our principal at that time did her best to pacify the parents and even arranged for a separate session for parents with the facilitators. I don't think it worked.

Sex education in schools or homes cannot really be effective in isolation, just as our children cannot be reared in isolation. Parents and schools need to trust each other and work together for the well-being of children. So, if you're a parent who is hesitant about sex education in school, ask for a meeting and talk to the school about what will be taught and how. Ask to see material and information on trainers. Voice your concerns respectfully and please remember that schools that are including sex-positive, non-judgemental sex education, probably have the best interests of your child at heart.

Grow a funny bone

I have always been the serious kid in the family; the one who watched The X-Files with glee and thrived on novels instead of comic books and music. In short, I was simply not prepared to deal with a little boy who was extremely imaginative in the scatological (yes, there's a word for all obscene fart/poop imagery) department. Although I enjoyed my fair share of naughty jokes in college, nothing, I mean NOTHING prepared me for the insane interest that kids have in all things smelly, gooey and disgusting. And not surprisingly, all of these have some connection with our bodies. They're either coming out of them or entering them or simply being spat and gurgled as practice, of course.

So, I felt rather sorry for myself that I was to be stuck alone in the business of raising a very scatologically inclined little boy after my divorce. After much wallowing in self-pity I decided to become the 'cool mom'—the funny, weird, crazy mother who comes up with fart jokes and blows bubbles on tummies and makes weird, pig noises to make kids laugh. It was difficult, because as soon as the children know you have these tricks up your sleeve, you become very popular with them and then there's no respite from them! But it turns out that has its perks too. I am the absolute favourite aunt on both sides of the family and the boys think I'm so gross that I can actually sit in on their closed-circle meetings! I also get to be the first one who hears all the crush stories, kiss tales and period mishaps. That is no mean achievement for an adult.

All this fooling around and goofing off doesn't mean that I don't take what the children share with me seriously. What it means is that these little people find it easier to connect with me and tell me or ask me things that they might otherwise find daunting to share with or ask another adult. Humour is the language kids understand intuitively. They are born to laugh and giggle, unless we beat all that joy out of them with decorum and seriousness. There's a time for those too, but that time is not every time. Growing a sense of humour around awkward things helps make them normal. If kids know that you are okay with sharing fart jokes and silly stories, they will also trust you to ask anything that seems confusing to them, especially things about the body.

Your laid-back, humorous attitude will also make it easier for you to set boundaries for them when it comes to bodily curiosity and queries. A parent, who usually laughs and jokes around, is more likely to be heard with seriousness when required, rather than a parent who is always solemn, stern or sombre. That can make things terrifying and difficult. So, if you weren't born with a funny bone in your body, grow one! Hoard up on funny things to tell your child when she comes from school, and voila! you will immediately become her confidante with whom she will share all the funny and not-so-funny things that happened during her day. One silly joke a day keeps the chatter in sway!

It will be untrue to say we need to respond carefully, tenderly, sometimes humorously, only for the child. We also need to do this for ourselves. The moment we let go of our draconian notions of judgement and morality, we create huge cushions in our relationships with our children—cushions we can fall back on when the going gets tough, warmth we can hold on to when we're upset and angry with each other. It is part of our job as parents to create these comfort zones, so our children feel motivated to seek us, question us, even annoy us, when something they don't understand about their bodies happens. And in this challenging, yet fun, process, perhaps we'll be reminded to look at everything through the curious, joyful gaze of children.

Chapter 3

Puberty

Tell me, tell me mother mine,
If my body sprouts a forest and there flow rivers of red,
If my heart flutters like a sparrow and I have strange thoughts
in bed,
If my eyes begin to dream things I like, but wouldn't be caught
doing dead,
If everything seems fuzzy and confused in my head,
If I become fat or hairy, or if I turn dark or thin,
If I looked too different or if I looked just the same,
Would you still love me, mother mine, or would I fill you
with dread?

It is interesting how first encounters with bodily changes at the threshold of adolescence set the tone for how we relate to them for the rest of our lives. If you encountered puberty as a shock, as a development that you weren't trained for, chances are you'll feel out of control about most things pertaining to your body. It is probable that you'll struggle to feel comfortable in your own skin and will have to learn to treat your body with kindness and care. Perhaps that is an over-generalized statement and perhaps I shouldn't be making it; but most of what I share here comes from my own experience and I understand that they were similar to the experiences of most people of my generation. I remember being a scraggly, ten-year-old girl in class five. I didn't even look much like a 'girl'. I loved wearing shorts and had short-cropped hair because I couldn't be bothered to care about it. Besides, not breaking my thick-lensed glasses every week being an achievement in itself, I could outrun most of the boys in my neighbourhood, including my older brother. I had no sense of being any different from them in any way except for my ears. They had been inadvertently pierced by my grandmother one day when my mother was away at the hospital. It was around this time that I'd had my second encounter with blood.

The classroom benches had just been painted a thick, russet brown and we had been sent out to sit in the field until they had dried. I don't really remember whether it had been summer or winter; perhaps it was a bit of both because I remember wearing a light jumper. I remember trudging back to class for a drink of water and absentmindedly sitting down on a bench that was still wet. Darn it! Now there'll be a stain. But who cared when there were so many exciting things going on, looking for freshly fallen *imlis* from the tamarind tree in our field being one of them. I didn't even bother to check to see if my skirt was stained.

On our way back to class before dispersal, I remember our class teacher, stopping me and asking me to turn around.

'What's that on your dress?' I followed her gaze to the back of my skirt.

'Oh, that must be paint, ma'am, from the benches,' I replied nonchalantly, skewing the skirt of my white frock around to check. And sure enough, there it was, a deep-rust-coloured stain that faintly resembled the shape of Australia with tentacles.

'It's not paint,' she replied stonily. 'Go home.'

Huh. I *was* going home. And what on earth did she mean 'it's not paint'? What else could it be?

But my class teacher had already stalked off. I collected up my schoolbag from class and commenced what I still refer to as my 'walk of shame' to the school gate. I will never forget those twenty minutes from when I exited class to when we left for home. Every older girl who saw me giggled and every teacher who passed by me, stared. What had I done? No one bothered to help or solve the mystery of the paint stain for me.

Eventually, the Lord had mercy on me and my older sister appeared, quickly assessed the situation and ushered me outside, hurriedly fastening her sweater around my waist. That, my dear friends, is how I learned about menstruation; suddenly, shockingly and shamefully.

But that's okay now, because my 'walk of shame' is also the reason my ten-year-old son knows all about menstruation. That's the reason he knows all about monthly cycles and sanitary pads, he sometimes even runs and fetches one for me when I forget to take one to the bathroom. That is also why he pays enough attention to sanitary pad commercials to inform me that the pink ones are better than the green ones 'because they won't itch, Amma!'

He doesn't look away uncomfortably, waiting for the advertisement to pass. He also knows that he needs to help and not giggle, if he ever sees a girl in class with a tell-tale, red stain on her uniform. It gets even better—and I feel prouder—he sensitizes all the boys in class about how to respond if a girl ever complains of stomachache and needs a pad. All the boys know how to be discreet and helpful and that a hot-water bottle and a first-aid box with sanitary napkins is essential classroom equipment. I like to believe that the women in my son's life will always feel comfortable and cared for around him.

Sometimes, the 'walk of shame' used to flash in my mind when I first began to notice my son's body change and grow. I would remember my fright and shock at what I thought was a violent illness when I was told that my body had changed forever. I would remember feeling humiliated, lost and lonely when my mother told me that I shouldn't let anyone touch me down there. I realized then that I had already been touched that way and that this sudden blood was somehow connected to that feeling of being hurt, being stolen. And I never ever wanted Imaad to feel that way. I wanted him to be prepared, I wanted him to accept and welcome his growing body.

I would look at the twin daughters my close friend has and wonder whether they knew, and whether they are prepared. I decided not to wait until they asked. I didn't want them to experience the trauma of being a stranger in one's own body. I wanted to celebrate when they would come to me and tell me they've had their period. And they did tell me, because I decided to grow a voice; a funny, friendly, warm voice that refused to be silenced or embarrassed because others may find it uncomfortable. I taught myself to find age-appropriate words and books and share these with the kids around me. I decided to become the cool mum, aunt, cousin, godmother who talked about everything! I trained myself to celebrate each change in my son's body, to call out for ice cream when he found a few strands of thick, black hair growing on the 'squishy' thing beneath his penis and yelled 'hair!' from the bathroom. I even pulled up my sleeves and showed him that I too have armpit hair when he said that he thought it was gross.

That may seem excessive to some, but it was and is important for me to be this way. I am a single mum with very few adult males around me with whom Imaad has a strong bond. I know there will be a time (older teens close up about personal issues and that is a natural part of their individuation process) when he will be too uncomfortable to talk about his body with me. I wanted to do the best I can to normalize growth and change for him now and later, to even celebrate it. I wanted him to love his body, to appreciate it, to not fall victim to modern 'standards of beauty' that expect us to shave, wax, thread, bleach, cut, everything that is pronounced ugly in the glossy magazines full of airbrushed pictures. I didn't want him to go through the process of learning how to be 'body positive', because that would mean there was a time when everything about his body felt 'negative' to him. Most of all, I wanted him to not detest his body, like I did, for years.

I will cut short this rambling homily and tell you why I put this in here in the first place. If you're parents, especially if you're parents with growing children, all of these reasons and resolutions quoted above, must become your resolutions too. We cannot shy away from the fact that our children are growing, that their bodies will one day not need diapers but sanitary napkins and condoms. We cannot ignore the fact that their sweet voices might one day sound unpleasant or screechy and they will begin to have erections in sleep and fantasies that are sexual. We cannot pretend that they will never have crushes, never need bras and razors or learn the actual physical meaning of the term 'masturbate'. We cannot live in a nursery-rhyme bubble forever, believing that 'my' child will never be curious about the opposite sex or want to kiss and date. Because chances are that this will happen, whether you find out about it or not. And if you have a pre-teen in your house and you think it's not happening, you have probably no idea what is going on in your child's head or maybe he or she is too afraid to share. I can't decide what is worse, not paying enough attention, or not inspiring the confidence and warmth to have an open relationship with your child.

As much as we'd wish we could jump straight from when they're small, babbling tots to when they're sensible, sorted adults, we can't skip this part. I know it's hard to become the kind of parent the likes of which parade around with funny comebacks and cool jokes on American sitcoms. It is difficult for us because we've been brought up in a culture where it was not the parents' job to talk about menstruation or pubic hair. In fact, it was nobody's job. We were all just supposed to somehow breeze through it without any help. But we did take help. Sometimes it was sneak peeks at *Grihshobha* magazines, sometimes it was pretending to be invisible at our mother's chai parties and overhearing whispered conversations about elopements, affairs and girls who wore 'high' heels and therefore developed 'low' moral standards. As for boys, learning was often limited to who had the 'biggest' penis and who could spray urine furthest in school bathrooms. Not the best way to learn. That's probably why so many of them are still stuck in the competitive mode (and so many of them end up asking if it's 'big enough' in bed when they're older).

If we were lucky to have parents who worried about our puberty at all, an older cousin would be roped in by them to tell us the 'basics'. This wasn't always a good idea either because older cousins can be annoyingly condescending and very capable of making you feel like an ignorant insect. More often than not, somebody who is not emotionally invested in your well-being won't be able to go about a sensitive business with empathy. I remember my distant aunt who was visiting then, sniggering at me and whispering to everyone in the house that I had now 'become a woman' when I got my period. I hid in my room and wept until my mother came home from the hospital, where she worked, and taught me how to use a pad. But not even she explained to me why I needed to use a pad at all, or why my knickers were stained with blood. All I was told was that this was something that 'all girls go through' and that there'll be bleeding for a few days every month. Nobody explained why! To a child, there are few things more gnawing than unexplained whys. They can grow into monsters in childish brains—monsters that can mean anything from deadly diseases to bodily alien invasions.

And, thus, the monsters grew, until the day we encountered that other monster called 'The Reproductive System' in middle-school biology class. As it was, our biology teacher wasn't a friendly specimen. Everything in her dress code, from her *bindi* (the sticker dot in the centre of an Indian woman's forehead), to her sari, matched perfectly, but we were often left wondering if she had cut out her heart and preserved it in a glass bottle in the lab. The class, when the chapter was taught, was an inchoate mess of giggles, cold stares and clipped explanations; none of these in the least bit reassuring. I remember the detailed diagrams of ovaries, the uterus and the male reproductive organ and how there were eggs and sperms but none of us could understand how things really *worked*. What went where, what came out and from where, and so on and so forth. Asking questions was out of the question unless we wanted to be ridiculed and embarrassed in front of the entire class.

Since I'd had the dubious honour of having gotten my first period in the presence of everyone in my class, I became

a guru of sorts and we spent the next few weeks after that
scary class discussing the mechanics of menstruation and
ovulation and all sorts of '—actions' with the entire class
huddled around me under a tree in the basketball court. That
impromptu tuition class earned me the title of 'Guru ji' within
my circle of friends and I'm afraid I was guilty of passing on a
lot of misinformation, but the title stuck. Despite that, I think
I was one of the lucky ones for whom having a period was not
all cloak-and-dagger stuff to be kept hidden within the family
and from the world at large, neither was I ostracized from the
kitchen or banned from eating certain foods. Perhaps that was
because both my parents were doctors. There were girls who
couldn't go into their pooja room or attend tuitions. Then there
were girls like me and my sisters who pretended to fast while
we weren't fasting because we were on our period. We had
to feign it because the world and the gods needed protection
from the simple biological fact that a girl was menstruating!
What about the boys? They were left struggling to make sense
of all this giggling secretiveness while their own voices turned
into croaks. Their defence mechanism was making fun of girls
and each other, coming up with horrid jam jokes and never,
ever telling anyone about how they were feeling because well .
. . *mard ko dard nahi hota* (real men feel no pain), and 'mards'
were what they were evolving into.

Things have changed a lot now and the children of today
know a lot more than we ever did. But do we know how to
discuss these changes with our kids—changes that mean growth
and beauty, strength and vulnerability, the power and the fear
of an adolescent child teetering on the threshold of adulthood?
How do we, as parents, lead the way when it comes to preparing
our children to take care of, and understand, their rapidly
changing bodies? How do we ensure that our children's bodies

never become a source of shame to them? How do we teach them to not pass off period stains as dried paint and breaking voices as a sore throat even as they worry in silence?

We talk to them. About developing breasts and itchy pubic hair, about wet dreams and period cramps and above all—about remembering how beautiful and welcome all of this is. Let me share some things we need to remember while discussing puberty with our children.

Puberty is not just physical

Interestingly, nothing that we read in textbooks or overheard and discussed had any context or subtext of emotional changes and feelings. Feelings that made you feel confused in your body or unsure about what you were experiencing or why. As parents, it's our job to keep our kids safe physically. And it's also our job to be the compass to the emotional tides that churn within our children, especially when they are sudden. Puberty is not just about the physically obvious, it is also about huge hormonal changes that are happening within the body. These may cause irritability, sleepiness, aggression, anxiety and most commonly, a hazy confusion about feelings for the other sex or for the same sex. The latter may become more confusing with the lack of information around gender identity.

It's not enough to talk to children about menstruation or nightfall. We also need to talk about internal emotional changes that they may experience and how to cope with them. Everyone who was ever raised in a household where puberty was never openly discussed knows that it can be a very difficult time. If a child doesn't know what's happening to them, if there is misinformation or information laced with guilt and shame, things can get out of hand quickly. One minute you're a happy eight- or nine-year-old child and a few weeks down the line, you feel differently about everything. Being with friends of the opposite sex, or even the same sex, may start feeling weird. Blushing, sweating excessively, body odour, feeling attracted to someone without knowing why can feel very inconvenient and frustrating. Your own body begins to feel foreign, everything you knew about it begins to change. Some teachers begin to suddenly object to regular things like boys and girls laughing and playing together, hugging and holding hands. People make girlfriend-boyfriend jokes where earlier everyone was just friends. Suddenly you have all these secrets inside where everything used to be transparent. This can be a daunting experience for the bravest of children.

As loving, committed parents it is our job to prepare children for puberty and its concomitant emotional upheavals before it actually occurs. Instead of an abrupt conversation after something happens, discussions and facts need to be introduced slowly from the age of seven or eight. It is important to talk about all of this in a manner that is completely natural and devoid of any secrecy or vague allusions. If we introduce puberty as a change that needs to be hidden or kept secret, we introduce shame. Of course, some families may choose to stick to modest clothing or not-so-open discussions about certain things. But talking about the body as if it's sinful can lead to long-term damage for children, even impacting their sexual health and well-being later in life.

Don't just talk to your daughters, talk to your sons as well

For the ostriches amongst us parents, it is easy to ignore signs that don't scream for attention. But we can hardly keep our heads buried in the sand when a daughter starts bleeding at puberty. We reluctantly disclose some information, however embarrassed or awkward we may feel. Boys lose out in the bargain because the changes in their bodies aren't quite so obvious. They are subtle and slow, unlike for girls, who suddenly blossom into young ladies overnight. Most mothers will somehow manage to have a conversation about puberty with their daughters and it is assumed that fathers too will talk to their sons about it. But that's the problem, it is only an assumption. Father-and-son relationships have never been encouraged to be open and friendly in our culture. Most fathers tend to be strict authoritarians who often inspire obedience and fear but seldom affection and friendliness. Exceptions do exist, but this is what we generally see. Most father-son relationships are fraught with undercurrents of subtle hostility and even resentment where sons either challenge their fathers or rebel and disregard them altogether.

Small wonder then that more sensitive topics, like nightfall or the sudden sprouting of hair in body parts that one didn't even realize existed or sexual fantasies and masturbation, are either completely ignored or perfunctorily mentioned. If you dig deeper into your own family histories, you'll often remember this amusing game of tag played between parents about who should talk to the son about 'such matters'. I believe it is only the boys who lose out in this game of unnecessary embarrassment. These boys grow into confused young adults who find it hard to seek help when confronted with intimacy issues or sexual-health problems because they've never been encouraged to discuss things openly. Suffering in silence may lead to frustration that very often affects more than one person.

Most boys never quite learn to interact with girls in healthy, equitable ways post-puberty, or to understand consent and respect boundaries. Femininity befuddles them and girls appear as mysterious as a forgotten secret language. Add to that the Indian tendency to segregate girls and boys into separate boxes as they grow older, and we have a generation of men and women who think the other sex is an alien component. No wonder the Mars-Venus concept is so popular here! Sorry to disappoint, but we do belong to the same planet and all that's missing is the healthy encouragement about seeing each other as people first and not about boy-friending or girl-friending everything. It's not uncommon for parents to ask a little boy if he has a 'girlfriend' yet, and the little girl whether she has a 'boyfriend'. While there's nothing wrong in that happening at an appropriate age, introducing romantic ideas about the other sex too early robs children of their capacity to relate as children and equals first.

We need to talk to our boys openly, warmly, in a language they will understand for their long-term health and development—both physical and psychological. Otherwise, most boys will only have access to misinformation that reaches them through their peers and more dangerously, through pornography. For them, porn sets the standard for sexual interaction, where pleasure is male-oriented and everything is about performance and aggression and not consent and mutual pleasure. Gradually, popular culture, crude jokes and toxic depictions of masculinity turn everything tender and beautiful about sexuality, first crushes and relationships into vulgar power play.

How will our boys ever develop the ability for emotional connections unless we help them establish it? How will our boys know how to value self and others above academic and material achievements unless we teach them to do so? Puberty is the ideal time to reinforce sensitivity, not just towards themselves but also towards others. Raging hormones and restless energy often leads to clashes and bullying in boys. A better understanding of what is happening inside their bodies and how it manifests as anger and irritability can help boys to find alternative methods of managing disagreements. Try and discourage violent video and other games based only on violence. While competitiveness may be a hardwired trait in most boys, it need not manifest through rough handling of other kids or bullying. Encourage empathy from a young age by praising every small act of kindness and sensitivity towards others.

We relentlessly limit, reprimand and prohibit our daughters from things that we feel will lead them to harm and hurt. But we hardly, if ever, teach our boys to limit their reckless reactions and hyper-competitiveness that often lead them into trouble. Boys need just as much direction, loving care and understanding during puberty as girls. If we take the easy way out, by not informing boys of the pubescent changes of adolescence and letting them figure it out on their own, there will be one of two outcomes. Either they will bite off more than they can chew and flounder in a morass of self-inflicted problems or completely shirk all responsibility. In both cases, it is themselves that they damage the most.

Crushes are joyful

One day, not very long ago, my son came home from school and related this refreshing incident to me: 'Amma, Yuvraj said something strange today. He told me that whenever M (a girl in their class) enters the classroom, the temperature seems to rise. Can that really happen, or is Yuvraj going bonkers?'

Sigh. The beauty and thrill of first crushes, that subtle dance of butterflies in the stomach and the prickle of heat on the neck at the sight of that someone who suddenly becomes special! What wouldn't I give to be ten again, besotted with that blue-eyed demigod who my cousin brought home one day. Just looking at him made my heart do cartwheels (only, I realized later, that it wasn't my heart, but my hormones!). Prehistoric as it may seem, let's not kid ourselves and pretend we never felt any of these things as young boys and girls in school. I don't know about you, but I certainly did! And if you have no memory of the charming bliss of first loves then I extend my sympathies; you missed out on one of the most beautiful, innocent aspects of puberty and adolescence—crushes.

I wonder why they were termed 'crushes', but then I think it is an eminently apt description of adolescent attraction. All common sense is crushed right out of you, and all you can think of is how her cheek dimples when she smiles or how his hair seems to swim when he runs. That extra minute to set hair just right even as your hapless mother screams at you to hurry up, plaits abandoned in favour of fluffy ponytails and absolutely no hair oil on school days—such are the extra measures that crushes demand. And in our hurry to be parents and sensible adults (the two seldom go together if you ask me), we hurry, scold, rush and shame our children out of this beautiful phase of their lives.

Adolescence is that in-between stage where your child is still a child and not yet an adult. Their sense of self is rapidly expanding to include those outside their immediate circle of comfort. The body is not just a curious tool anymore. It has been examined and used to explore the world, but now the attention strays out of this close circle of knowledge. The strong emotions that puberty brings on lend a rosy colour to everyone who seems attractive. It is as if young boys and girls on the cusp of teenage see themselves and each other afresh. They are more than playmates, more than just classmates but less than something defined. Newly minted in each other's consciousness, they egg curiosity and attention, like diamonds sparkling in the sand. And all this is perfectly natural—shy giggles at the mention of a certain name, the insistence to wear perfume when a certain friend is visiting, selecting one's own clothes and choosing styles that no longer resemble the pastels of childhood—all of this is perfectly natural. What makes it unnatural and embarrassing is our reaction to how our children change during this time.

There was a magazine for children called *Target* when I was growing up. It was my window to the world, to different cultures, trends and books. In my desert of a city, there wasn't much to do for growing kids. There still isn't. So that magazine was my monthly outing. It took me to places I had never been to, and I got to know people I would never really meet physically. This was made possible through a thing called pen pals. Most kids today wouldn't understand what this means but for us it was the equivalent of texting, albeit a lot slower. *Target* had this little guest section where people who wanted to make pen pals left a note and their address (telephone numbers being unfashionable then) and those who wished to write to them could do so. There was a letter by a boy called Inder (name changed). He was thirteen and he liked Egypt, snails and rivers. I was eleven and I liked Egypt too. We started writing to each other; charming little letters full of drawings, paper cuttings and sometimes, even shells. We wrote to each other for months until one day my brother (sorry, *Bhaiya* (brother)!) discovered one of his letters, opened it and read it. He showed it to my mother and together they decided that I couldn't write to Inder anymore. At the end of that fateful

letter, he had inscribed these words, 'I love you, Reema.' And
this was his sin and my punishment. I never even got to keep
that letter. It was torn and thrown away.

I wonder where Inder is today, what he does, whether he
has children. I will never know because two adults in my life
treated my feelings inconsequentially, they read things into
that letter which had never even crossed our young minds,
and above all, they chose to act for me. They took away
something that was precious and innocent because of some
unnamed fear that made them feel that this was dangerous.
Letter writing, texting, calling and meeting friends with firm
boundaries in place is not dangerous. What is dangerous is
our paranoid fear that our children have grown minds that
want to be free of our absolute control. What is scary is the
way we limit and punish our children while trying to protect
them. Protection can only come with trust. It's not something
you can ensure with the tearing of a letter or the confiscation
of a cell phone. It's a safeguard that is built from infancy by
sharing openly about what is safe and healthy behaviour, what
is appropriate and why.

You could say that I'm being naive, that crushes today
can very quickly transform into pre-teen sexual encounters
and that is unwise. I agree that the onslaught of sexualized
messages from the media and too much availability of
information at the mere click of a button has added ominous
dimensions to erstwhile innocent encounters. But that has
happened only because we choose to make relationships,
sexuality and puberty look dangerous to our children. We
do this with such subterfuge, force and vehemence that our
children stop coming to us with their questions and concerns.
When that happens, we've left the door wide open for them to
fall into experiments that might hurt them and relationships
that could rob them of their innocence.

Therefore, oftentimes it's our own fear and not our children who are responsible for the crossing of limits that are in place for their own safety. When we consciously replace harsh words and tones with warmth, in a way that make us accessible to our children, when we replace admonishments with joyful banter about special interests like a new crush or a latest fashion trend, we create a home where a child feels accepted and not ashamed. It becomes easier to talk about boundaries and respect when we ourselves demonstrate this to our children and show them enough respect to not label them for anything they say or do.

I will never know what became of Inder, but I do know which girl in school my son likes. We talk about her. I helped Imu buy a present for her birthday and never, ever teased him when he shared that she thinks he's very handsome. I ask him what she looks like, and he finds her picture from the online school birthday board and shows it to me. I tell him that she looks like an intelligent girl and I remind him to treat her with respect. He tells me he dare not cross any line with her because she'll whack him, but also that he would like to kiss her someday.

'When we're older, Amma,' he tells me. 'We're too young, no? She's special but she's not my girlfriend and anyway, I'm not making a girlfriend until I'm sixteen.' I smile and cough a little fake cough, 'All right, all right, eighteen, then! You're so old-fashioned, Amma! But you will let me take her to a movie before that, won't you? And is it okay if I text her from your phone for homework when I miss school?'

'Yes, of course, Imaad, a hundred times yes. Because crushes are special, and they make for beautiful memories when we're older. I wouldn't deny you the joy of having a crush for any misplaced fear. Because I trust you and I know I have taught you well. And even if you do something that may seem unacceptable at first, I will take the time to understand you, to talk to you, because you're not fully grown yet. You're still learning.'

Puberty—More awareness and support

For a lot of children, adolescence can also mean increased anxiety about their sense of self which might usher in a lack of debilitating diffidence With new pressures to fit in, including appearance and behaviour, some kids may feel out of step with the world and look for reassurance from people and places that are not very safe for them. Research on child abuse, bullying and cyber-crime has shown that children who tend to seek validation from outside their trusted circle are more susceptible to being victimized through false praise and sympathy. It's easier to get sucked into a vacuum if one feels ungrounded. I wish fewer children felt this kind of instability but the more I look around, the more I see that we're just not attuned to how our kids feel.

One of my closest friends is a brilliant woman, full of creative ideas and a stellar work record, but all her life she has listened to this one voice in her head, her mother's. Despite achieving considerable success, she always second guesses herself and is very rarely sure of her worth as an individual or a professional. We've often discussed this and it turns out her childhood was replete with negative criticism from her mother. Nothing she did was ever good enough; nothing was praiseworthy or credible. My friend says it impacted her to a degree where she needed constant approval from friends and teachers. I can only imagine how easy it could have been for anyone to groom her or bully her through false compliments and praise. One might argue that our parents were strict because they didn't want to spoil us; being soft has only led to a generation of kids who swagger around feeling entitled. While I agree with some of that in terms of material benefits that are so easily available to kids today, I do feel that the old way of using negative criticism and harsh punishments created a sense of worthlessness, rather than discipline, in our generation.

Children who are assured of their worth, valued with not just words but also actions, are more secure and less vulnerable to abuse and harassment from potential abusers or bullies. There is nothing like parental love to build a solid foundation for a robust sense of self in children. Your voice is the voice they will hear in their head all their lives and they need your words and actions to affirm and encourage them, especially at puberty. I cannot tell you how many clients I see who still have a bodily-trauma response to memories of names they were called by parents while growing up. A lot of them have a loud self-talk that repeats dialogues that their parents would say whenever they did something that was perceived as a mistake.

Those harsh voices never really leave their heads:

You're good for nothing.
You're useless.
You're lazy.
Don't you have any sense?
You'll never succeed.
You're a failure.

These are some of the parental statements seared into memories of individuals as adolescents, reducing grown adults to tears in my office or zoom room. Our worries and our fears for our children's future or safety need not manifest as cruel words. You can be aware of who your children are interacting with and where they're going without suffocating them. Look out for them, assure them that you have their back and will support them no matter what or who they feel threatened by. Please tell them that they are beautiful and unique and no losses can dim their brilliance. In a world which values material wealth, academic performance and physical beauty above everything else, your children should have the courage to be happy with the way they look or what they have. And you and you alone can give them that.

I often catch my son eyeing himself in the mirror, pulling up his T-shirt to look for 'abs'. He says he wants an eight-pack abdomen like Tiger Shroff and I jokingly remind him that his mother has a 'family pack', and that's okay. As he grows older, I see him being more and more influenced by the way people look, what they wear, what they have. I know that's only natural. I remember a time when I used to hide in my bedroom when we had guests because I thought I was ugly. No one called me that, it was just that there were too many beautiful people around, too many outsiders comparing me to others and not enough people telling me I was okay the way I was. Yes, we need to talk about health, fitness and education, but not in a way that makes our children feel inadequate. Because, if they begin to feel small, they will withdraw inwards, become invisible and compel themselves to fit more tightly into whatever box is marked appropriate. Upholding them no matter what they do is not the answer, but maybe softening your tone as you correct them when they're wrong may just be the key to raising well-balanced children who will know how to stand up for themselves. God knows we need that now more than ever, with our world becoming scarier by the minute.

Talk about diversity and inclusion

My mother asked me this morning whether I was gay. The question didn't matter to me; it was the expression she had on her face that did. As if being gay was as bad as having cancer; a communicable cancer. So, you're worried if your kid is dying and worse, if she is going to transmit that death disease to everyone around. I don't blame my mother, I don't judge her either. She was born and raised in an environment where there was no knowledge of gender identities that could be different from the normative man and woman assigned at birth according to what one had between the legs. She's seventy-three years old. I can hardly expect her to change. For me, it's enough that she's even asking me this question.

That expression is simply not acceptable for you and me—parents raising children in this day and age. We don't have the excuse of not knowing enough about gender, sexual identities and choices to judge, shame or punish our children, or others for not being normative heterosexuals (in other words, the type of children our grandparents would have been happy to raise). This is not easy for me to believe, much less write here, for my whole *khaandaan* (family) to read and then judge me. But I'll do it anyway. My God cannot punish people for the way they choose to dress, love or identify. My God is as vast as the universe; even more. I'm sure a little rainbow is not too inconvenient to accommodate within that vastness.

As parents, who give birth and nurture life, I ask you to try and emulate that vastness in the way you see your children and pass on that vision to them. Because if you don't, you'll join the ranks of those who have forever hurt, shamed, limited, disowned and even killed those who differ from most people in their choice of dress, sexual and gender identity. Remember that tomboy in school who dressed and behaved like a boy? Or that boy who seemed to like other boys? *Mittha*, they used to be called in my father's days. It's funny how openly you can talk about things with your loved ones once you let go of fear. My father says boys like that were ruthlessly ragged in hostels, even violated and they couldn't report or complain because it was somehow their fault that they were born different.

I went to an all-girls' school and it was not uncommon for girls to have crushes on each other. In case you didn't know, that's perfectly natural adolescent behaviour, especially in a cloistered environment. But sometimes things got a little intense and therefore, scarier. A girl in my class used to sit behind me and touch my hair. I didn't mind, she liked my hair. She was always nice to me and went out of her way to help. I knew she had a crush on me and that was fine too. She hardly made me feel uncomfortable. My own fascination with her long hair and beautiful eyes made me uncomfortable. It took me a while to understand that it was okay to admire her like that. What wasn't okay was how the entire class took it upon themselves to point and whisper whenever she came to talk to me. My friends even told me to stay away from her because she was 'bad—one of those ones.' But she didn't do anything bad. She was just the way she was, a little different from the rest of us.

It's the difference that most people can't stomach—the fear that there's someone out there unafraid to own who they are, to be how they want to be. Their natural ease with their identities (however fraught they may be on the inside) hit us like an accusation. We are reminded of all that we hide for fear of censure and ridicule, we are reminded of how we diminish ourselves because we want to fit in. And therefore, we point, accuse, name and pointedly ignore those of us who dare to be different. They could be females experimenting with androgynous clothing, or trying to assert their sexual identity, or boys who like other boys and are afraid they'll be misunderstood. They could be someone from a minority community, labelled with hate and derogatory names. They could be someone with a disability or mental illness. They could be one of the children from your neighbourhood. Or your own child even!

So, talk to them. Even if it's just out of care for your own child, because you wouldn't want anyone to judge them or be nasty to them because of how they look, walk, talk, what they wear, who they like, what they worship or eat. If it's just for that, talk to your children about expanding our hearts, including all colours, all choices in them. Teach them to try and understand even if they don't like someone, to try and empathize. And the only way you can do that is by demonstrating how to accept wholeheartedly, love deeper and understand more fully, those around you. The best way to teach children anything is to do it, to be it.

Chapter 4

Sex and Reproduction

'Amma! Why did Hermione and Ron have to kiss?
They ruined the movie!'

If you haven't had a quiet afternoon of reading or a leisurely cup of tea interrupted by a sudden, breathless question that includes that three-letter word a lot of adults love thinking about, and children are mystified by, you have missed out on the greatest awkward bomb moment of your parenting life. SEX. That word. In young children, it arouses the same mix of fright and fascination they feel while looking at pictures of giant monsters—squishy, scary, yet very, very interesting. And their keen desire to understand the mechanics of sex and reproduction can make for very healthy doses of laughter in families. Or extremely awkward silences, rushed explanations and even chiding or punishment—depending on what a family's disaster-management technique is.

Every parent I know lives in mortal dread of the moment when their children will eventually decide to upturn the humdrum routine of everyday life with that one question— what is SEX? Following, or followed by, other alarming questions—like the one above. That one followed the kissing scene between Hermione and Ron in a *Harry Potter* movie. The magic of kissing (and *Harry Potter* movies) was ruined for me in that moment with that question. Sigh. I am no different from most parents, even though I talk about all sorts of uncomfortable things the same way I'd ask for sugar in my coffee or buy vegetables every morning. But when it comes to one's own child, all that bravado and confidence just seems to whoosh out. You're very aware of the fact that you're probably the only person who means the world to your child and therefore, everything that you do and say has a lasting impact on your child's consciousness. Well, no one said it was going to be easy!

Consider this—your child comes home from school one day with a stunned look on his face. He avoids you the whole afternoon and just when you've managed to ignore the feeling that something is amiss, he comes and whispers in your ear, 'Amma, what is S-E-X?'

In that moment, you know that life as you know it, has changed forever. Out it comes—all the love-making scenes chanced upon accidentally on TV, dogs and cats seen mating as they screech and howl, the whispered conversations in classrooms and four-letter words scribbled on grade four desks. Little minds whirring with absurd explanations. The best one I've heard to date includes describing sex as 'the mummy-daddy workout'.

Then there's the question of babies—screaming, bawling and forever pooping siblings and cousins. Where did they all come from? Why are they needed? When I was in grade six, we placed bets on how babies 'happen'. As long as I'm alive I'll never forget what one of my friends, Rati, thought she knew was the correct answer. 'You pop a pill, simple!'

According to her, 'When you want a baby, you go to the doctor and tell him. The doctor then gives you a medicine which you take with water and the baby begins to grow in your tummy. Just like you plant a seed, okay? When it's ready, the doctor takes it out. It is really very simple.' Apparently, the whole process was not only very mechanized but was also conveniently inverted to avoid any uncomfortable truths about two bodies exchanging fluids. To make matters worse, she hadn't cooked up this explanation herself. Her mother had told her this! I understand her mother's reluctance in answering her daughter honestly, but I can't help wondering if misinformation is helpful for young people.

I don't think our parents really knew how to answer questions about babies and sex because . . . well, they belonged to simpler times when such questions occurred late to children most of the time. And any discussions around biological processes relating to relationships were simply taboo. It was just not allowed to discuss sex or reproduction, especially in the context of pleasure. I think it's extremely rare to find anyone in their thirties today whose parents talked very openly or whose grandparents ever discussed this topic with their children. One may call them ignorant, or unaware, but the truth is that those were very different times, at least in our country.

It's never easy for any parent to acknowledge the fact that their children are growing up. Because accepting it also means accepting the fact that they'll have to relinquish all control over their children's lives and let them explore the 'big, bad world' on their own. And that's a scary thought. I consider myself a very eager-to-let-the-little-birdie-fly mother, but even for me, the thought that someday I will no longer be able to protect my child from the real world is frightening. And yet, one must learn to let go. Perhaps answering life's awkward questions without squeamishness, with humour, with examples from the natural world and subtle references to family, love, bonding and shared parenting is one of the ways we can learn to let go and teach at the same time. Who knows, in the process we might even learn to sidestep an awkward bomb with all the dexterity and grace of a seasoned ballerina! Let's give it a try and look at the aspects we need to consider while discussing reproduction and sex with children.

House rules about all things 'sexy'

Assuming that you have thought and talked about parenting methods with your partner (if you're raising a child with one), I think it would be safe to say that you have probably also discussed your perspective on how to talk about sex and sexuality with your children. It is okay if you haven't done that yet, but I feel that it is important to be clear about things that might be influenced heavily by your religious or moral values. In our cultural context, how we interpret religion and morality still has a huge bearing on how we expect our children to behave, especially in terms of creating and sustaining relationships.

While it may not matter to some Indian parents, I believe the majority are still not comfortable with the idea of pre-marital sex, masturbation or other means of sexual exploration. Every adult has a right to exercise the choice that they think suits their needs but, as parents, we're more comfortable setting boundaries that are acceptable to us. I think it becomes important to discuss these boundaries as a family with growing children in a healthy, open manner where you lay down your expectations from your children while also giving them room to express how they feel.

I believe it is not realistic or fair to expect complete compliance from your children when it comes to things like what is the right age to have sex, or when you believe that pre-marital sex is sinful or shameful. I know that I have differed from my parents' views on these things with age and we have found a way to agree to disagree about personal choices to keep the peace. But that has only been possible with the understanding that every adult in the family has a right to make personal choices and that should be respected.

If we become too rigid in the enforcement of our values about sex with our children, chances are we will eventually encourage them to rebel or hide things from us, which may put them in more danger than when we know about what they're doing. Being open about how to practise safe sex, contraception, consent and responsibility decreases the chances of youngsters finding themselves in dangerous situations which may not be entirely reversible. You get to discuss things and lay down your thoughts and ideas about sex, dating, kissing, etc., but please understand that children are hardwired to test boundaries and all of us have felt the urge to push limits set by our families as young adults. The only way we can give our children room to explore life safely is to create a warm, interactive environment in the house where there is room for discussion, negotiation and listening.

So, talk to your partner about how and when you'd like to start discussing sex with your children, if you're okay with them dating and at what age, how openly will you talk about safety, emotions, reproduction and relationships with your children or if you want to discuss all this in terms of religious rules and boundaries. You decide how much is too much but do keep in mind that children grow up to be individuals and your job is to guide and help them, not control them.

The XYZ of babies

It's all because of the cats! And the dogs, the pigs and all the other mammals who regularly flash us with their very public displays of (not just) affection at all times of the year. It's a free country and I am an ardent supporter of the 1970s 'love everywhere' philosophy; but really, the sight of two dogs locked in a post-coital embrace by their bottoms, accompanied with suction sounds is too much to explain to young children! The easiest thing that comes to you is a very simple explanation about 'how they're making babies' and all the screeching, caterwauling, nipping and sticking to each other in weird positions is all part of the 'mating game' which animals and most humans indulge in when they want to make babies. At least that's how I explained it to Imaad when our two cats suddenly seemed completely obsessed with each other's behinds, sniffing and licking each other. Thank heavens our ardent animal cousins believed in oral sex! I almost envy the lady fellows. Sigh.

'Why is Tommy putting his little pinky into Maya, Amma?'

'Why are they howling like that?'

'Where did I come from? Yuvraj said that we come from the place our mummies pee from. Chee!!'

'Why is Khaalajaan's tummy growing round, Amma?'

'But how can a baby live there? How did he get in there in the first place?' etc., etc., etc.

Questions like these became standard in our house when we brought two kittens home four years ago. As luck would have it, my older sister decided to get pregnant at the same time and came from London to stay with us. Very inconvenient, I tell you. Boom! Our household became a minefield of (re-) productive question-and-answer sessions which inevitably started with big, loud 'why's and ended with even louder 'But show me HOW's'.

In the beginning I was a little alarmed and worried that Imaad was too young to understand reproduction clearly, but when I spoke to my friends with children in the age group of five to seven years, almost all of them shared similar experiences of children being very inquisitive about where babies come from or how they're made. Perhaps it was the next stage in their curiosity about the natural world. In most cases that curiosity followed the arrival of siblings and/or pets in the household where they saw tummies growing rounder and mummies returning from hospitals with squeaky little babies and pets giving birth to tiny litters. It is but natural that curious children will ask questions about things they have never seen before so closely.

I put my own experiences together from the time when I was pregnant with Imaad and the children around me started asking questions when my pregnancy became obvious. One wanted to know if the doctor would have to 'cut' my tummy to take the baby out and whether that would hurt. Another wanted to know where the baby came from and yet another wanted to know how the baby breathed inside my tummy. I wasn't sure about how much their parents wanted them to know in terms of the human reproductive act, but I was sure that these kids were naturally and imaginatively curious. There was a certain delight about their curiosity which I didn't want to extinguish by saying squelching things like 'I can't tell you, ask your mum' or 'You'll find out when you grow up'. Answers like these close down conversations with a child and break the innocent trust that a child has placed in you to ask that question in the first place. In a culture where asking questions is not really celebrated, it takes courage to find a voice to ask anyway. I'd rather we cherish the curiosity and intelligence that children have and find easy explanations supported by examples from the natural world to answer them.

That is what I did, both when I was pregnant and surrounded by loving nephews and nieces who clung to me, and also when my son came to me for answers—I used the questions themselves to provide answers and took the moments as 'teachable moments', to set aside my own discomfort to respond to them. To put it differently, every time a child asks you an awkward question, you're saved the trouble of looking for an opportunity to bring up reproduction and sex. It can be a little perplexing to think about when the right time is to introduce these topics and some parents may become too serious and preachy if they go about this as a separate lecture exercise that is not blended harmoniously with daily life.

So, if a child has asked you a question about how babies are made, half your work is done! That doesn't mean that you sit around waiting for your child to ask! If your child hasn't displayed curiosity about reproduction and sex on their own by the age of six, I suggest that you look for little windows where you can introduce the topic yourself. You could do it on a trip to the zoo, while watching a show that has babies in it, while visiting someone who has had a baby recently, while playing with pets or when you find a little bird or a nest or simply while making an omelette! Although I think your child will refuse to eat eggs, accusing you of being a 'murderer' if you use breakfast-making as an opportunity to explain how hens have chicks!

Here's how you can use simple phrases to explain reproduction to young children without going into too much detail or using terms that will cause confusion. Answers should stay as close to the questions as possible. Too much information can cause confusion. For example, you don't need to explain menstruation, sex for pleasure or ejaculation to a very young child to explain how babies grow in a mother's tummy. That stage will come later, around puberty. In the beginning you can stick to broad facts.

- Making babies is like a kind of dance for most animals and humans. They kiss and cuddle to make a baby together which grows in the mummy's tummy until it is ready to come out. Sometimes we need doctors to help the mummy bring the baby into the world.
- Some animals grow their babies in eggs which are kept warm to help the baby inside grow. The egg hatches when the little baby is ready to come out.
- Babies can breathe easily inside the mummy's tummy. It's like people can breathe while swimming. The baby also swims and sleeps inside its mummy's tummy. You can tell that the baby is growing as mummy's tummy grows bigger. When it is ready, mummy and doctors help the baby to come out. Sometimes it can be painful for the mummy, but we can all help mummy feel better by taking care of her and helping her.
- For some animals and all human mummies, babies come out from a place called the vagina. It is like an

elastic band hole that stretches to help the baby come out. It's not the same place where girls pee from but it is close to it. No, this is not dirty. Human bodies are not dirty. Things like peeing, pooping and having babies look messy, but it's natural. We clean ourselves, shower and change our underwear to stay clean and healthy. Some animals lick themselves and their babies to stay clean. We use water, soap and shampoo to stay clean. It's the same thing. (Use similar examples to make things easier to understand.)

- We need both a mummy and a daddy to make a baby because daddy and mummy are equal partners. You need two people to make a baby and raise a baby (that's reproduction and gender equality rolled into one!). Daddy helps to put the baby in mummy's tummy and mummy helps to grow it inside. Both need to help and work together to build a family.

- When children ask exactly how daddy 'puts' a baby inside a mummy, you may briefly explain it like this: when we grow up, our bodies change to help us make babies. But you need to be grown up and sure that you want a baby. If yes, then daddy puts his penis inside mummy's vagina (I'm hoping we're all naming private parts with kids! It can't work otherwise, folks. Buck up!) and they make an egg together. I understand that this can be hard for most parents to say out loud and I'm not saying that this is the only right way to go about a situation like this. But I do feel that misinformation and half-truths sometimes do more damage than good in the face of exactly 'how' questions. If this is too much for you, you can say things like mummy and daddy love each other with their bodies and that makes an egg in mummy's tummy. The egg then grows inside a sack-like home inside mummy's tummy. It keeps the baby warm and healthy until it is time to come outside.

- For those of you who plan on introducing same sex partners and parents to your children, you may say things like: some families don't need both mummy and daddy to make a family. Some families may have two mummies or two daddies and that's okay. Babies need love to grow and if the parents have love, it doesn't matter who they are. They bring a baby who doesn't have a family home and raise it with love and care.

- Even if you don't plan on talking inclusively about gender and different family structures, please be aware that at some point, your children will come across unconventional partnerships and family structures and you will need to put some thought into what you want to tell your children. My values are based on mutual love and respect, irrespective of gender and I explain everything in those terms. My family may choose to disagree with me on this, although those are not my values.

- If you want to explain relationships, sex and building families in terms of religious guidelines, please make sure that you use explanations and not fear to pass on your values to your children. In my limited experience, explanations based on love for self, others and God make more sense to children. Fear does what it's supposed to do—scare and drive away.

Breathe. Think. Speak.

There's no one way to discuss sex with your children and it's impossible to tell if they'll ask you before you tell them or vice versa. Chances are that if you have a healthy, open relationship with your child, he/she will come to you for explanations even when they have received information from outside the family. For the sake of ease, I will share my own experience with my child here to explore the possible ways and nuances one needs to keep in mind while responding.

When my son was nine years old, one afternoon he came to me while I was reading and whispered in my ear, 'Amma, I need to ask you something, please don't be mad at me. What is S-E-X?'

That is exactly how he said it, spelled out one letter at a time and in a low conspiratorial whisper, as if we were discussing where to drop the next nuclear bomb. And it didn't feel like any less of an explosion inside my head. My first impulse was to run screaming; to wish my little one were a newborn again and a long way away from all things grown-up. But I didn't have that luxury. I'd rather have him hear about important and not-so-important things from me rather than from his friends and Google. It was time to bite the bullet.

My book and phone were put away as I drew my son closer and reassured him that he could ask me anything and I would never be mad but, before I answered him, I told him I'd like to know where he came across the word. The story that followed made me feel fearful and proud in turns. My son went on to tell me that his partner in school had told him all about sex, rape and f*****g and that he watched videos at home that showed how it's done. He said that one of his brother's friends had told him it was cool to kiss and have sex and that he loves doing 'it'. The said child's brother's friend was thirteen at the time. I was horrified!

But this was not the time to talk about my child's partner or what he knew. I had to focus on what I felt my child should know—that sex is a normal adult activity that two grown-ups engage in when they are very close and want to express their love for each other and also when they want to make babies. I told him that sex is meaningful and beautiful only when the two people involved respect and trust each other and are both willing to 'make love'. Of course, he wanted to know exactly HOW it was done and I explained briefly, but my focus was on explaining the act of sex in the context of consent, love, respect, pleasure and most importantly, adulthood. That brought on more questions of why kids shouldn't do it and why it was important to wait until you're grown up: so that you're safe from infections and are old enough to responsibly care for babies if you want them. I tried to avoid talking about contraception because I felt that it wasn't needed at the time.

Some things can't be avoided however, and I had to go back to what my child's friend had said about rape and watching videos on his iPad. My son had some idea about rape. He felt that it meant 'torturing' girls and that it shouldn't be done, and I had to explain to him that 'torture', in this case, had more to do with forcing sex on somebody and not just hurting them. As for the videos, it was important to talk about how the way sex was shown in videos was not real and that it was not okay for kids to watch stuff like this. He seemed to understand that and told me that he had tried telling his friend that it wasn't good to watch everything on YouTube and that if his mum found out, he'd be in trouble. But his friend had laughed him off and called him '*darpok* (coward)' and had said that no one could stop him from doing what he wanted. I tried explaining that maybe his friend was just curious and needed a grown up to talk to him about his screen habits.

There are a few important things that I learned from this unnerving exchange. I understood the importance of being affirmative and honest with one's children as it brings you closer to them and they begin to tell you more about how they perceive the world. Over the course of the next few days, we had several interesting conversations that ranged from how babies are made, what sanitary pads are used for, where babies come out from and even blood relations, second marriages, stepfathers and stepsiblings. I got so many opportunities to delve into my little one's curious imagination, his fears, his insecurities and his uncanny ability to understand complex concepts with natural ease. I was offered a wondrous chance to lay down the foundations of one of the most beautiful aspects of creation in the context of love, sensitivity and respect and I took it. I was reminded of the fact that fear is often the beginning of good things.

I also learned first-hand about the dangers of exposing our children to too much before they're ready to understand contexts and meanings and how kids can often use teasing, taunting and humiliation as a way of getting their peers to try something new. I was worried and afraid about how naturally the other child had accepted pornography as natural and real when it is anything but that. I felt like I needed to get in touch with the other child's parents and talk to them about their child's experiences. I tried to do that through the school but they didn't give out any information about the parents. I asked them to inform the parents and bring the child in for counselling and a healthy conversation but I'm not so sure that happened. Unfortunately, most schools aren't interested or equipped to handle any issues that might not be connected to the curriculum or teaching methods. We can't fix everything but what we *can* do is speak to our children.

The most important thing I learned from this whole experience is that, when the birds and bees decide to buzz at you, you should buzz right back—cut down all the noise, create a safe space and listen so that you can be heard too.

Masturbation

The interesting thing about masturbation is that everyone who has any authority over you, the school, the scriptures, your parents, your elder brother, your raspy old Buaji—everyone tells you not to do it and they still do it in secret. Grinding and sweating to whatever arouses them—pornography, the latest item song and, for those of us born in the 1980s and 1990s, pin-up posters of our favourite stars, either shirtless or bosomy. Everyone will tell you that if you do it too much, your penis will become weak if you're a boy and that you'll become oversexed if you're a girl. Worse still, they'll tell you that you'll become impotent or that no one will marry you. I've even heard a boy say that 'it' falls off if you masturbate too much! They'll say all this and still do it! That's the thing about human beings, they can be kind of mean and don't want you to have a good time. And parents can be mean too, not out of spite, but probably because they know how pleasurable and distracting masturbating is. And we don't want our kids having fun, do we? Right?

Wrong. Dear, darling parents, your kids will masturbate, whether you like it or not. And they will get to know of it before they can actually do it. Because the human body is designed to experience arousal after a certain age and your little boy or girl will chance upon the thrill of pleasure possibly while swishing down a banister, or from an accidental rub or maybe for no reason at all. Because that's how it is with the human body; it has a mind of its own. Even if your child doesn't actually experience arousal and self-exploration, she will most certainly come to hear of it from that pernicious grapevine all parents dread for more than one reason—the school. And there's no stopping that grapevine once it starts buzzing. So, I'd say we clear the air before that happens and talk to our kids about self-pleasuring when or after we talk to them about sex.

There's no way of knowing when a kid will ask questions about sex or masturbation and which questions will come first. But it's good to be prepared to discuss openly and without judgement by the time they're eight. I know that sounds alarmingly young, but with the explosion of information around us, early exposure is a given. It's best to be ready. And when I say ready, I don't mean for you to make a list of cold facts, but creating a consistent practice built over time that makes room for unexpected questions. That practice best evolves when we remove our own biases and judgement, making room for enquiry as a natural process of growth.

One interesting thing about how masturbation is perceived and talked about is the distinct, yet subconscious, gender stereotyping we colour it with. While it is considered normal and even cool for boys to self-pleasure, there's a lot more secrecy and censure around girls pleasuring themselves. I believe this is an effect of female bodies being denied agency and control while traditionally being viewed as instruments for male pleasure. Most cultures, especially our culture equates female sexuality with promiscuity or 'loose morals'. There is very little room for young girls and even women to discuss, explore and express themselves sexually. More often than not, while boys are quite open amongst themselves about sexual exploration (even to the point of bragging about it), girls often condemn and judge each other for sexual expression. Such is the intensity of our conditioning to see females as devoid of any sexual agency and conflate that with morality, that women themselves are blind to the restrictions imposed on them by tradition.

And, when the time comes for our daughters to grow and enjoy the power and beauty of their bodies, we inflict them with shame through sharp edicts on the way they should dress, express, love, learn and grow. There is simply no room for them to become aware of their own sexual preferences and needs, to learn to negotiate those needs safely and without pressure or to even feel at ease in their own bodies. I believe what we say to our children when it comes to bodies, pleasure and sex and the way we say it should be free of judgement and shaming for both boys and girls. We have had enough of strait-jacketing our daughters into being mere receivers of sexual experience, denying them self-expression, sexual and reproductive health rights.

We cannot say that our boys and girls are equal until we grant them equal space to learn about how their bodies work, how they can enjoy and take pride in their strength and beauty while staying safe. So, if you're ready to talk about penises and semen, please be prepared to talk about vulvas, clitorises—that hidden power-house of sexual pleasure that every young woman has a right to own without any shame. It is not for us to weigh our children with labels that violate their claim to all kinds of freedom. Our only job is to make them as aware as possible so they may learn to assert their rights while keeping themselves and others safe.

Talking about consent and boundaries is IMPORTANT!

When I was nineteen years old, my then boyfriend told me he wanted to kiss me madly. I remember feeling a rush of panic and pleasure. But the panic was decidedly more pronounced. There was something in the way he implored me, told me he loved me and cared for me that made me believe that letting him kiss me wasn't such a bad thing after all. I let him kiss me and a lot else besides. I liked it, yes, but I wasn't ready. I remember feeling confused and afraid afterwards. This was love, it was supposed to feel right and yet it didn't. What I didn't know then was the fact that I was allowed to say no and wait until I was sure of what I wanted and whether I even wanted it at all. Before I could understand the difference between sexual desire and a genuine emotional connection, I had committed myself to a marriage that was fraught with complexities to begin with. I never gave myself enough time to understand my own desire or to embrace the nuances that float between romance, love and lust until after I was divorced. Maybe that was one of the reasons we separated; we did not know how to speak the language of disagreement gently, yet firmly.

So, when my son and I came across a movie scene where a hero was repeatedly tugging at a heroine's *dupatta* (a long scarf), following her and imploring her to be with him, I took a pause. I asked my son if he felt that what was happening was right. Did the girl look comfortable with what was happening? Was it okay for the boy to follow her and push her to 'say yes'? My son was confused.

He said, 'But, Amma, everything is okay in love, no?'

What he said is testament to the way we have been taught to act in love, the way love is presented to us in song and word—love as a powerful force to which one must bend one's will; a force to which one loses one's individual voice. This version of love and relationships has no room for individual doubts, for respectful breaks that ensure that everyone is comfortable, so that everyone can say 'no' to something that they're not ready for.

A lot of the confusion that young people feel around consent and how much they're okay exploring physically and emotionally has a lot to do with popular portrayal of relationships in media. Take the notorious movie *Kabir Singh* for example. At every step of the way in the movie, the male protagonist literally hounds the female protagonist. He declares her to be 'his' even before she really knows him; he pulls her out of her classroom forcibly; touches her without asking permission; and all of this is portrayed as passionate romance, even when he hurts her emotionally and physically hits her. What is worse is that the heroine responds to this behaviour lovingly. When kids grow up watching this, they learn that calling someone '*mera hai* (mine)' or '*meri hai* (mine)' gives them absolute authority over that person's being, both emotionally and physically. And also that, when someone does that to you, the right way to respond is affirmatively. It's not surprising, therefore, that a lot of boys and men find it hard to accept emotional and sexual rejection. They grow up on a steady diet of media that teaches them that it's their right to have anyone they want. And young girls watching this can internalize that this is what relationships are like and they're supposed to be okay with it.

Peer pressure and the fear of being rejected are other reasons why young people find it hard to articulate their boundaries. Teenagers feel pressured to experiment sexually and it is common for them to brag and ask each other who has done what sexually. For those who may not feel entirely ready to explore sexually, this can be daunting, and they may feel pressured to do things they might not really be okay with. Especially when they first start going out or dating, be it seriously or just for starters, there is often a silent expectation of sexual intimacy. Most young folks, especially women, may feel like they owe the other person kissing, making out or sex because they have taken them out, or shown them attention. Our youngsters need to know that dating and sex need not go together. That it's okay for them to hang out with someone, to take their time being comfortable around that person and then see if they want something more. What most teens also don't know is that it's okay and even healthy to have conversations around what kind of intimacy they're comfortable with and what they would like to be careful about. Of course, this can be embarrassing and awkward but learning about consent is as much about being okay with awkward conversations as it is about articulating what they like or dislike. And I feel kids can learn to be okay with discomfort and awkwardness and see value in it if we initiate, guide and pace such conversations at home.

One important aspect of consent that is very hard to understand and even harder to internalize is that consent can be withdrawn or revised. In the wake of the Me Too Movement, a lot of cases came to light where the alleged accused argued that the victim had agreed to sexual activity in the beginning and that they assumed that she was okay with whatever happened later. A lot of victims responded by saying that they either changed their minds later because they felt uncomfortable with what was happening or the dynamics of the relationship with the accused changed and they no longer desired sexual, or any other, intimacy with them. Now this sounds very cut-and-dried on paper. But revising consent in between interactions can be both hard to give and hard to accept or understand. Non-verbal cues and body language have been traditionally accepted as consent when it comes to intimacy but for the sake of safety, clarity and comfort, I feel that clear, verbal consent given or taken by asking clear questions and asking them with a clear yes, no or not now can help. Even experts agree that consent is a very grey area and is hard to pin down in relationships or interactions that are dynamic. Which is why it becomes all the more important that we discuss consent with our kids, especially teens.

These are some practical ways in which you can practise teaching consent:

Start when your kids are small—Consent is not just sexual. It can be taught to very small kids during play and interaction with other kids and even you. From the time children are born, they are taught to give in, to heed and obey everything but their own internal voice. By the time they are adults, they have learned to successfully ignore their discomfort at anything, especially in relationships. Because relationships (romantic or familial), they have been told, are paramount. They deserve sacrifices. All of this is bludgeoned in with twice the force and traditional logic if the child is a girl being raised to fit into the roles of a sacrificing daughter, wife and mother. For boys, expressions of emotional hurt are criticized and they are often told that they are being too sensitive for a boy. This can lead to their struggling with saying how they feel and defining boundaries around unpleasant behaviour with others.

The flip side of this is that a lot of children, especially boys, are not asked to stop when they're hurting someone or mind how they play or talk with other kids. The argument '*baccha hai* (he's only a child)' condones all kinds of teasing, manhandling and rough play, especially between siblings. Kids therefore learn that there are no boundaries, and they can get away with anything.

Common arguments supporting boisterousness can often sound like:

'Brothers tease sisters. That's how they show their love. Why are you making a fuss?' or

'She just pinched you, it's a small thing. Why are you crying so much?'

Gendered messages mixed with a refusal to acknowledge a child's pain can convey both messages: It's okay for someone to hurt you and you should put up with it and it's okay to ignore someone else's pain or discomfort.

When your children are young and you notice that they don't pay attention to the discomfort of a friend, a sibling or a playmate, who doesn't like something being said or done (like hair pulling, pinching, pushing or name calling), please intervene and ask your child to listen.

You can say things like, 'When someone says they don't like something, you need to respect that and stop. It's not okay to keep doing xyz when your friend says he/she doesn't like it.'

When a teacher, friend, family member or playmate repeatedly hurts, offends or does something that your child is not okay with and it comes to your notice, please step in and speak up for your child. It can be hard to do especially when it's things like a family member pushing your child for a hug or a friend teasing 'harmlessly'. But to a child, watching a parent intervening and telling off anyone who's making them suffer reinforces a strong message: my feelings matter, I have the right to protest and say 'no' and I have the right to be heard.

When we force our kids to play with kids who continuously hurt them or to show respect to a teacher who uses mean words, it's as bad as our telling them 'you don't matter'. We are separating them from their intuitive voice that tells them 'this is not okay'.

Creating a healthy listening environment indirectly reinforces consent—The underlying strength behind being able to say what one is really feeling is knowing deep down that differences—of opinion, of choices, of likes and dislikes, wants, needs and desires—are okay. Too often we criticize children for voicing their opinions because they jar against our own opinions or maybe they sound shocking. When we label and shut down kids for expressing how they feel about an issue or a choice, we indirectly send the message that they are irrelevant. Kids who grow up in environments where differences of opinion, especially around personal choices like clothes, hairdos or friends are not tolerated and judged, may have a really hard time standing up for themselves later in life.

We learn to honour ourselves when those around us in our earliest years honour us and show us respect. If a parent coerces, emotionally blackmails or forces children to do what they think is better, what the child imbibes is that 'relationships mean we do as others say'. And that directly feeds into how much we're able to create boundaries or say no when we are older, be it in friendships, groups or romantic relationships. Consent, or lack of it, is easier to voice when we have solid memories of being able to say what we like or don't without being rejected by our parents.

Too many clients come to me with concerns of not being able to set healthy boundaries with authority figures, not being able to say no to friends and lovers when they don't like something or want to skip something like a social event or gathering. When I probe deeper into where these patterns might have emerged, in almost all cases, they stem from being around a parent or parents who severely reprimanded, withdrew love and attention and/or gaslighted the child when they said or did something that was against the parents' wishes. That often leads to people-pleasing tendencies where kids find it easier to go along with whatever is being asked of them even if they don't like it, rather than being able to decline. That childhood memory of rejection, hurt and abandonment runs too deep.

I encourage you to treat disagreements with your children with the same respect you would offer when disagreeing with an adult. If your child chooses something you really don't like or does something that you consider offensive, you can respond by saying things like, 'I disagree with this,' or 'I don't like this', focusing your response on the behaviour or action and not on the child personally.

Saying things like, 'If you do xyz, I will not talk to you,' or 'if you do xyz, that means you're a bad child', focuses attention on the child personally which can feel like rejection. It is likely that this will reinforce pleasing behaviour in your children even when they're not okay doing or saying something. So, your child's choice to wear only black doesn't mean they don't appreciate the coloured clothes you buy them; their insisting on a mohawk haircut or hair colour or a tattoo doesn't mean they like to upset you or go against your will. The fact that they may not like reading like you do or cooking like you do, does not mean they're not appreciative of who you are. If they don't like talking to a nosy relative who asks personal questions or makes comments about their grades or appearance, doesn't mean they are disrespectful. It simply means that they choose different things, and they want to set certain boundaries with people and that should be okay.

Set boundaries for yourself too—Parents, especially mothers are traditionally expected to be self-sacrificing. Everything from their time, their interests, social life and entertainment takes a back seat when children appear on the scene. And perhaps that is needed in the early years of an infant's life for them to feel secure and surrounded. But as kids grow older, sacrificing your alone time, whatever it may be, sends the message that whatever you're doing or whatever you may need is not really important. Most children cannot pick up on cues easily about what you may need when you're sick, upset or overwhelmed by work. And we hesitate to tell them because we feel we owe them our full presence, time and attention. But when we push ourselves to be there for them even when we are running low on steam, we increase our chances of being irritable, snapping at them, shouting and even hitting. It is better then, to teach growing children to respect your limitations or for them to be okay with your taking time to read a book, taking a long shower or going out with friends.

This can sound like, 'I am really tired and I need some time to relax. Is it okay if I take a long shower and can I request you to please not knock unless it's an emergency? Mommy needs to feel fresh. I can play with you later.' Or 'I'm sorry I can't play with you right now; I have a bad stomach ache. Can we play something that will not strain me later?' Or 'I haven't seen my friends in a while, and I miss them. I am going to do xyz with a friend and I hope that's okay with you. I really appreciate this.'

This can all be hard to communicate to young children and can be met with tantrums but with gentle reinforcements, and as they grow older, kids can learn to respect your need for time, space and recreation. What they learn by watching you do this is that it's okay to do things one wants or needs even when others may not agree. It's a direct lesson in self-care, setting boundaries and honouring our needs. All three are important for growing kids to learn and express later in life. Also, when you will sometimes say no to a child's demands when you're not feeling up to something, you're also teaching them to respect boundaries; important lessons in terms of acknowledging refusal. And all of us know that this doesn't mean we say no to something that is really important to a child or necessary for their safety or well-being. Saying no here is more in terms of teaching them to accommodate your needs too. But please remember, just as you expect them to respect your boundaries, please be willing and open to respect theirs, especially around privacy, personal space and touching.

As parents we can re-negotiate the thin lines that separate disrespect from voicing opinions, adjustment to other people from repression. We can go back to our childhoods and rewrite each incident where we gave in for the sake of love, respect or tradition at least in our minds.

We can unlearn and re-learn so we can teach our children that love, relationships, sex and life in general has room for doubts and differences, discomfort and boundaries. That way, we communicate to them that everything is not okay if you feel it's not okay for you, no matter who you're with.

You can't (and shouldn't) escape talking about porn

So, we have talked to our children about sex, we have told them what to do if someone touches them inappropriately.

We're happy and smug in the knowledge that we're ready. Until. I thought I was ready until the day Imaad showed me a crumpled slip of paper which had the following note written on it, 'xnxx.com watch this it is so much fun.'

My son was nine when he brought home that slip. The child who gave him that slip was also nine. I'm not sure I have felt more apprehensive about parenting than I did at that moment. I had in front of me an invitation to go on the world's biggest free-porn site and I didn't know what to say to Imaad.

Should I tell him porn is bad? But I have watched it too, even as I struggled with the guilt that came with it, because anything sexual was explained to us in the context of sin as children. The truth is, most adults watch it. It is a source of sexual gratification for many people. A lot of people don't have partners to have sex with. Pornography is their only source of pleasure. Kids watch it because everyone else is watching it and it is new, it is exciting. All of us have gone through phases of obsession with porn, trying to find secret ways to watch it. From renting out video cassettes and circulating it in friend circles to painstakingly waiting for that first porn video to download during the early days of the Internet, to deleting our browser history on smart phones just in case our spouse or kids catch us, we have ALL watched it. But we like to pretend we haven't. All this and more clouded my mind as I grappled with what to say.

And then it came to me. Pornography is not real. It is a performance much like other forms of visual media. It's an act devoid of the warmth and love that constitutes real relationships and more often than not, it functions from a place of male power over the female body. If I wanted my son to understand porn is unhealthy, I had to explain it in these terms. Not in terms of sin and fear that had been handed out to me. And those edicts invoking divine wrath could neither curb my curiosity, nor could they limit the sneaky desires of all my friends. I trust that is how youth will continue to function. We learned, experimented and messed up our sexual relationships because our point of exposure was either unreal and mechanical or excessively romantic. We didn't know anything about expecting equality in the bedroom, using communication to increase intimacy or to know how to negotiate discomfort. We learned through trial and error and sometimes, through horror.

I am sure that my son, like so many other kids will experiment with pornography, but I don't want that to be something he or other kids learn from. Or the place from where we disseminate knowledge. Popular representations of sexual relationships warp our understanding of sex and cause long-term damage to how young people understand and engage with intimacy. These representations need to be discussed as removed from the concepts of warmth, equality and consent, as mere fantasies and a means of self-gratification, not learning manuals. And, while we do that, it helps to use words that don't terrify our children, but comfort and explain. Therefore—

Don't wait—Start from a young age and, without mentioning porn specifically, make it clear that there are some parts of the Internet that are not meant for children, just like some parts of their neighbourhood, streets, the world at large, are not meant to be traversed alone. Simply put, it can be unsafe and confusing to visit every part of the Internet on their own just like it is unsafe to travel unaccompanied at night or wander around in unfamiliar areas.

Talk about the difference between making love and 'making hate'—As your children begin to understand more about sex, explain that there is a great chasm or difference between real life to what takes place on the Internet. At the real-life end, there's the intimate and mutually enjoyable act of making love which is tender and based on enthusiastic consent. At the other end, there is what Professor Gail Dines describes as 'making hate', which is often what online porn is all about. Making hate is violent, often accompanied by abusive language and gestures. It can physically and emotionally scar the partners involved—in most cases, women and underage children.

Explain the porn business—The porn industry makes money by seizing your attention, which it does by showing the most extreme, unrealistic, unpleasant practices that have very little to do with reality or are not as commonly practised. Young people respond well to empathetic connections and when they see the way the sex trade works, they realize that some of the women are abused, underaged or victims of sex-trafficking. They're not doing this for pleasure, this is an exploitative business. This gives them a logical reason to stop watching porn while also providing you with an opportunity to discuss creating more lasting connections with other young people, sexually or otherwise.

Talk about consent—Pornography encourages the idea that sex is always available, and no one ever says no. It encourages the idea that women are sexually available for the asking and that everyone will say yes to experimenting sexually. Even in the way the porn film is shot, there is very little attention to consensual participation or female pleasure. Most acts are coercive or downright abusive especially when it comes to hard core heterosexual porn where it's normal to see one or more men penetrating a woman violently or at the same time. As far as real-life women go, that cannot always be a pleasurable experience for everyone. Some people may enjoy pleasure that borders on pain and that is okay too, but the idea that mainstream pornography propagates is more focused on male pleasure and control of female bodies. It is no wonder then that surveys on what kind of porn women watch show that they are more inclined towards lesbian porn as that focuses on female pleasure, especially oral sex which is not a huge part of mainstream heteronormative porn.

I believe that when the time comes for young people to be sexually intimate, we should be coaching them towards mutual and enthusiastic agreement which is revisited at every stage of physical intimacy.

P.S: When I was revising this chapter almost six months after I wrote it first, I couldn't resist adding two very interesting incidents thrown at me by Mr Firecracker after he turned twelve.

Here goes:

Episode 1
'Amma, I get that masturbation means self-pleasure or self-sex, but how does one actually do it? *Maane, karte kya hain?*'

I would've had to be made of stone to not suffer a minor tremor in my heart when Imaad asked me this. There was a rush of 'Dear God, kill me now!' thoughts in my head as I fumbled with what to say. And then I said what needed to be said.

I told Imu that when one feels aroused there's a rush of blood to the penis (in his case) which makes it swell and grow. This is often followed by a desire to touch oneself and stroke the penis.

Naturally he had to say, 'But how exactly?' and there I was, sliding my hand back and forth on the top of the pen that I was holding and feeling extremely pornographic.

I also had to tell him that masturbation often ends in a release of sperm called ejaculation. I know some of you will feel that perhaps this was too much information. But in my experience, direct questions are best not avoided or averted with false information. We're setting the standards for how our kids will perceive self-pleasuring for the rest of their lives and it's sensible to not fill them with shame or ignorance.

When we were done, I asked Imaad if he felt the need to masturbate or if it had happened on its own. He made a face and said that he's 'not ready yet' and merely wanted to know because all the boys were talking about doing it. I chuckled to myself and heaved an inward sigh of relief. I'm a cool parent all right, but I really don't want my child to grow up this fast!

Episode 2

Okay so this is slightly more graphic. In the winter of 2019, Imaad came up to me and asked innocently, 'Amma, do people make noises while having sex?'

Amma has never been as gobsmacked as she was then. I answered politely, 'Yes, Imu, sometimes they do. Why do you ask?'

'Oh, I'm asking because you know Shubh, na, my friend? He said people make noises like ooh and ahh while having sex and we were wondering why they did that. *Isliye poocha* (which is why I ask).'

(Amma died. Period.)

The noises described by our dear Shocker Shubh (I can always rely on him to make my life harder!), were accompanied by suitably sensual actions. I was as entertained as I was surprised. But then again, nothing should be a surprise to parents of hormone-bombed adolescents. I calmly explained to Imu that pleasure is often expressed through voice as sighs and other sounds that are sometimes loud and it's perfectly normal. In a situation like that, all that is important is to remember to make sure that you're not accidently hurting your partner. And because we had already established the premise of sex as being consensual and loving in nature, this wasn't hard to do.

Imaad seemed to understand and even said that he was quite tired of his friends bombarding him with information all the time. He got up, sighing, 'All this will have to wait.'

I think I am secretly relieved at that.

Chapter 5

Bullying

I have often wondered what words would look like if we were asked to put a face on them. It's easy enough to imagine words like beauty, grace and sorrow. But what would the word 'crushed' look like? I had never imagined I would find this out until the day my son came home from school with a face that said, 'I'm crushed.' But within that crushed feeling, I noticed in him a ripple of anger that scared me. Fists clenched, cheeks flushed, eyes narrowed and his small chest heaving in painful, sharp jabs of breath that left air trapped somewhere in his throat. Something in my boy had erupted.

A classmate had called him a Pakistani terrorist in school. My son loves the Indian flag; he keeps it in his drawer. He believes in the idea of protecting the nation just as much as he believes in the fact that chocolate is the best thing ever. He is too young to know how flawed that idea is and I don't have the heart to give him a reality check just yet. His heart broke when he was called a 'bad guy'.

'I'm not a bad guy, Amma, I'm a good guy! I don't get into fights, unless a friend is being hurt.'

How could I explain to him that the child who called him names was not a bad guy either? That good guys and bad guys weren't labelled in stark black-and-white. How could I explain to my child that the other kid was probably confused and angry and wanted to hurt someone because he probably didn't know another way to deal with his angst.

I wish there were a simplistic, bullet-pointed method to explain the dos and don'ts of bullying to children.

- Is your child aggressive? Five things you can do to fix that.
- Is your child hitting classmates? Follow this easy method to curb this tendency.
- Is your child being bullied at school? Five things you can do to prevent that.

I wish it were just as easy for us, as parents, to know and hand out correctives to our children about bullying and being bullied. But that would mean that bullying as an issue is somehow neatly contained and limited to schoolrooms, buses and living rooms. I don't think we live and breathe in this world without bullying or being bullied by someone in some way or the other.

The Oxford dictionary describes 'bullying' in the following manner:

Present participle: bullying

Seek to harm, intimidate, or coerce (someone perceived as vulnerable)

From this perspective, bullying feels ubiquitous—almost as if I were a single word stranded, naked and alone on a blank page; I see it absolutely everywhere like the whiteness of that page surrounding me. Bullying runs rampant both inside and outside classrooms and in people's homes; it predates history and goes all the way back to the beginning of time. I see its baleful presence in the insistence of parents that their children study a particular subject or marry a particular person because those choices were considered more suitable. I see it in the quiet arm-twisting that goes on in marriages and intimate relationships where partners are emotionally blackmailed into doing something, with rage, tantrums or tears. I see it in schools where children are humiliated with impunity for misdemeanours such as being late, unruly or untidy in their work or being unable to meet the expected standards of performance in academics and sports. I see it in the government when political parties use any and all viable means to coerce votes. There is flagrant bullying in office cabins where bosses yell, upbraid, degrade and mark employees in circulars listing performance issues. Where and when have we not been bullied? And where and when have we not been a bully? And yet we seethe and rage when we get a complaint from school that our child has hit another student. We weep when our child tells us that he has been called a dirty name.

To examine bullying merely as a reflection of childhood issues is tantamount to putting a band aid on a bullet wound. A new term has emerged powerfully in the context of male aggression and violence—toxic masculinity. I understand that this is too specific and merely a tiny aspect of bullying as a whole, but let me use this as a starting point. Toxic masculinity is being described as a behavioural pattern in men that is demonstrated by withholding love, affection, attention and by using harsh words, teasing and physical aggression.

The phenomenon has been described as a direct result of emotional suppression in boys in their formative years by faulty parenting that doesn't allow room for boys to fully express themselves. It has been cited as the main reason for the emergence of this toxic behaviour pattern. That may well be true. I used to speak in the same terms not so long ago while espousing vulnerability as a necessary tool to rescue men from apathetic violence and pain inflicted on self and others. What is problematic in this whole discourse is that it suggests that toxic masculinity and bullying is an offshoot of faulty parenting and gendered notions of behaviour and that if we correct those, bullying and aggression will subside. Although that is partially true, I do feel like we're looking at only one page of an entire book.

As a new parent of boy/girl twins (at least as they were assigned at birth), I puzzle about the cultural pressure to scrutinise my infant son's burgeoning masculinity lest it emerge as 'toxic'. I catch myself watching and wondering, resisting the urge to police his interactions with his sister: He took the toy she was playing with, is this aggression that will stifle her confidence? She seems unbothered and has quickly snatched it back—phew! Is it bullying or an early form of manspreading when, both of them vying for the same object, he moves into her space and pushes her aside?

Today, popular parenting messaging, from Instagram to the *New York Times*, is suspicious of and concerned about boys. 'Boys are broken,' we are told. Boys underperform girls in school and college, and are more likely to engage in behaviour that is harmful to both themselves and others.

Boys fight, bully, take dangerous risks, and sexually harass.
From school shootings to incel-inspired terrorism, white
boys in particular perpetrate mass acts of violence.

If left unchecked, so the reasoning goes, these boys will
grow into gender dysfunctional men. Curiously, in 'toxic
masculinity' discourse, antisocial and poisonous gender
performances are the cause and effect of much of the harm
both faced and perpetrated by men. That the same basic idea
is the starting point for both pop feminist and men's rights
approaches to today's so-called crisis of masculinity is a red
flag that something is amiss with our framing.*

I think what Heidi Matthews is trying to do is highlight
the fact that the problem of aggression in children, especially
boys, cannot be simplified to gender roles and the way they
have been transmitted through generations. That this happens
is undeniable, but that this is the only cause for the way
bullying pervades classrooms and schools through boys is
not entirely true. I feel that patterns of violence, suppression
and coercion have existed long before these terms were
coined. Our evolution from a hunting gathering society to an
industrialized society where there was less and less room for
uniqueness has wrought tremendous violence on the human
race—for both men and women.

With the creation of factories where a huge mass of
people were expected to perform routine and repetitive
roles to achieve production goals, we began to be herded,
pushed and shoved in innovative ways. And then the modern
education system that was designed on the factory system with

---

*Matthews, Heidi, assistant professor of law, Osgoode Hall Law School,
Psyche (newsletter) July 2021, Canada.

uniforms, bells and performance schedules, created this mass suppression of individual expression in the name of progress that denied any individual emotion and trait to be exhibited freely. And propelling all of this, is the giant state machinery that seeks to protect the nation and to do so, creates armies of soldiers pushed beyond endurance, screamed at, shouted at, punished, to become the perfect soldier so that he may protect the nation perfectly. And what is the end of all this? Betterment, civilization, progress for all, sanctioned by all.

Performance at both the workplace and schools operates on the principle of exclusion. Who is better? Who gets more marks? Who is a better player? Who achieves more targets? It is a rat-race designed to reward the achiever and punish the slacker, thus creating very clear fault lines that identify the strong and the weak. In most cases, the 'weak' are the ones who don't conform to pre-calibrated standards.

In celebrating this idea of 'achievement', schools inadvertently create a system of those who have the power to bully and those who can be bullied. It is important to note that this power operates through mass approval and consensus. No one is powerful in isolation.

It is interesting to note that these exclusion structures that first began operating outside the confines of home were essentially male centric—factories, schools, armies, corporate hubs, etc., all of which began as male-dominated areas and were populated exclusively by men. Women became a part of mainstream education and the industrial and corporate workforces much later. For women, exclusion took on a different aspect.

With the advent of organized agriculture, some 10,000 years ago, farming became the strongholds of men, and women were relegated into domestic spaces where their importance and performance was evaluated with other exclusionary criteria. Women began to be valued and judged for their looks because the better-looking ones could provide more aesthetically pleasing offspring.

In a world where wealth and male status became irrevocably intertwined, the beauty, fertility and home-making skills of women became the benchmarks of status. Whose wife was more beautiful? produced more heirs? and kept a better hearth and home? Each of these threads taken separately will delineate the various strands of bullying that is common among female circles and young girls, even today: who is slimmer? who has the better-looking boyfriend? who is fairer? who is less contentious and who is more pleasant? All markers of women deemed more suitable as the perfect daughters, wives and mothers. And anyone who fell outside of these boundaries was, and is, a target. The sad part is that this form of exclusion is exercised not only from outside the female's domestic spaces but also from within.

Some of the worst cases of bullying in high school happen in girls' groups. They may not be physical or as obvious as when boys get into fights. But name calling, shaming and clique or group behaviour is more prevalent in girls' groups and schools. Just as some of the most violent acts of aggression on boys by boys happen within intimate groups of football teams, locker rooms, brotherhoods and neighbourhoods. The closer we are, the more we seem to hate and hurt each other.

When something is considered the norm, it gains enough traction to be weaponized against someone. When a certain physical attribute becomes popular, those who don't possess it are bullied. When a certain stream of study is considered more lucrative, those who choose differently are bullied. When an idea becomes more important than human beings, human beings are sidelined to promote the idea.

And who does this? Not one person or institution but the economy's class structures, beauty industries, nationalism, popular media, school boards, evolutionary theories. When the wheels of the world run on survival of the fittest, those considered unfit are trampled underfoot.

Therefore, when narratives of nationalism, fed by stories of valour, become the norm and that norm is fed to children as a characteristic of those who look a certain way, belong to a certain religion, support a certain political party, who are the 'others'? The others are those missing from these popular narratives, the others are those with unusual surnames and minority religious identities—just like my child became the 'other' in his classroom when another kid called him a terrorist.

Can I say with any certainty that this incident is an isolated example of bad behaviour and boys just 'acting up'? I can't.

The truth is that after the slanderous accusations, my son retaliated by pummelling the other boy, sitting on his chest and slapping him until the two were forcibly separated. So, can I now say that my son is mentally unstable and needs intervention? I don't think so.

All I can say is that both boys were playing out the scripts that are part of the larger framework of life and society. In that sense, did these scripts emerge only at home? And if they had, can they be corrected, rewritten and relearned only at home? According to Heidi Matthews,

> The popular idea that toxic masculinity can be both prevented and cured by instructing boys and young men in acceptable or healthy forms of masculinity is an unhelpful simplification. It offloads on to individuals the responsibility for countering the real problems of wealth and power distribution that lie at the heart of gender inequity.

Heidi adds,

> The core idea is that, with the right consumer choices (books
> on bullying, gender neutral clothes and statements) and
> anti-bullying protocols, parents and teachers can train boys
> and young men to be more in tune with their inner selves
> and their vulnerabilities. The deceptively uncomplicated
> premise is that this will then make boys more able to express
> their emotions rather than repressing them.

I remember having a conversation with my long-time
friend, R, many years ago. We were talking about slang words
and how children, especially boys seem to use profanity
recklessly. In the absence of an active spouse and father figure
for my child, I have often turned to my male friends and
cousins for advice. How can I decide what is good or not in a
certain context when I have never experienced that context? I
have never been in fistfights and slanging or sledging matches.
Maybe this was because I was in an all-girls' school and then
went to an all-women's college. Bullying in those environments
was more insidious, less obvious. So, when Imaad began to
show signs of loudly lashing out with either words or fists, I
didn't know what to do.

I remember R telling me that if I tried to sanitize the
way my son spoke to other children or if I forbade him from
indulging in a bout of fisticuffs, I would be creating a misfit,
someone who would be a prime target for other children.
I remember feeling aghast at the very idea and arguing with
R about it. How could I allow Imaad to scream profanities and
hit back in a fight with another child? How could I tell him
that it's okay to do that? And then R said something that has
stayed with me: 'You cannot insulate your child from the way

the world functions, Reema. Will you not send him to college? Will you never let him use public transport? Will you keep him incarcerated at home? No, right? If you take away all the words and actions that are popularly used in the way we relate with each other, especially boys, you will make the child stick out like a sore thumb and he will hurt so much more because of that.'

If I discouraged fighting, he wouldn't know how to defend himself in an environment where boys use violence to communicate. If I forbade him to use *gaalis* (profanity), he could be further picked on for being a prude especially in a world where clean language is often associated with the privileged classes. My brother had had some bad experiences because my family's perceived refinement and sophistication had made it difficult for him to establish a rapport with the other boys. To associate swear words and violence with lower-income-group demographics is to very conveniently ignore the fact that the worst violence is often found in the corridors of power and money. Abuse is channelled through mediums other than foul language in the homes of the cultured and affluent. Therefore, there is no saying that if my child is given to violence and expletives, he will become like the *gali ke bacche* (street urchins). The cultured folk who live their genteel lives in mansions are often the worst perpetrators of abuse and bullying. Can I, as a denizen of the mansion-ed elite, confidently claim that I have never really participated in any form of coercion? I don't think I can.

I remember asking R, 'What should I do then?'

I don't believe I arrived at a very clear answer then and I don't think I ever will. Bullying is a lot like an octopus—you cut off a limb and another grows in its place; you wriggle free of its tenacious grasp, you find another tentacle pinning you down. What I do have is a sort of a rough and meandering map of pathways we can tread as parents to support our children in a world that is not very gentle.

Not looking for single solutions

Oftentimes, when we are faced with a problem, there is the tendency to look for a simple cause-and-effect thread that will help set the record straight. Perhaps I could speak directly to the bully's parents. Perhaps I could ask my child to ignore the bullying and it will die down on its own. Perhaps the class teacher could punish the bullies and the incident will subside. I feel that everything in life has a butterfly effect and one thing is almost invariably and irrevocably connected to another in such an intricate way that if one thing shifts, everything moves as well.

In that sense, a bully at school is the way he is because of something unpleasant in his own background and environment. A child who acts out, pushes others and makes nasty jokes about someone else is trying to communicate something. It's a cry for attention or help. It is way more than the children involved in the incident.

When Imaad was in grade four, a classmate would often call him names and pinch him without any provocation. My child was understandably hurt and angry. I asked Imu to try and establish a rapport with the kid, to try and figure out if there was something going on with the child at home that was causing this kind of angst. In hindsight I think this was beyond the capacity of a child. But I didn't really know how to handle that situation then. Over the next few weeks, Imaad reached out to the child, offered to share his tiffin with the boy and made conversation with him. One fine day, Imu came home and told me that he had discovered something about this other boy. Noticing a bruise on that child's arm, Imaad asked him what had happened. The boy burst out crying and told Imu that his dad beat him almost every day. Something between the two boys shifted that day.

I reached out to the school quietly and asked them to keep an eye on the child. The school later shared that the child had a very troubled home life and there was little they could do to help him. But they did include him more in class activities and tried to show him more warmth. That child and Imaad eventually became friends.

This is not to say that we have to place the burden of reconciliation or understanding on our own children all the time. It's not on a child to be made to sort out another child's issues. But what we can do is bring some nuance and perspective into understanding a situation. That prevents us from knee-jerk reactions like reporting a child and publicly denouncing him. Most often, children ask their parents to not get involved because they know that any public incident will only make things worse for them at school or wherever bullying is happening. My sharing this is not to offer a naive solution to a formidable problem. It is merely a hope, a prayer if you will, and a sideways glance at things that stare us in the face every day, from so close that our vision blurs.

Placing responsibility fairly

When the Pakistani terrorist episode happened, I went straight to the school. I saw that the episode may be reflective of some oversight on the part of the teachers about what the students talk about, what news is shared in school and what religious messaging the students are exposed to at home and school. To my shock, I discovered that the principal had asked Imaad to ignore any derogatory comments, to not pay any heed to them and asked him to 'work on his mind'. A grown man asking a ten-year-old to use his mind to deflect abusive behaviour! It was too much to ask. I was livid and offered that it might be a good idea instead to conduct sessions around bullying at school and to include group activities in class to increase bonding. I also suggested that something be done about the way news and religious messaging was reaching the students.

I know that most of this messaging around nationalism and religion comes from homes but there is a lot that schools can do to create inclusion and acceptance in children. This school wasn't interested. When I pressed further, I was told that perhaps the problem was with my child. For a moment there, I actually felt guilty and somehow responsible for what had happened. It took me a moment to realize that I was the target of a classic, deflect-the-blame situation. I was determined to not let this slide. I emailed the owner of the school, describing the incident, copying in the principal and the class teacher, and demanded a meeting. I also hinted that if this wasn't taken seriously, I wouldn't hesitate to go to the press to talk about how the school was ignoring something this serious.

What followed was a series of meetings with the school during which they kept placing the onus on Imaad to ignore taunts and to keep his head down.

I insisted that this was an unacceptable resolution. I wasn't accusing anyone or demanding that someone be punished. I wanted a conscious effort to be made by the school to create awareness about abusive language and for the school to pay attention to complaints made to teachers by children that often went unnoticed. I was aware that it was difficult for teachers to take on yet another duty, but I couldn't see why something this significant could be the responsibility of ten-year-olds.

The entire episode made me vastly unpopular at school. However, on the upside, here's what also happened—no one asked Imaad to ignore things again; when I called the school, they paid attention; the other child and Imaad were put into counselling sessions at school together; we weren't sidelined.

Sometimes, when you kick up a fuss, schools will know that you are serious about the well-being of your children. And they will learn to pay attention not because you're thirsting for blood, but because you care about both your child and the other child. Even though this might not be the ideal solution, you'll know you have tried everything possible. Our children need to see us standing up for them and not standing aside while the child accepts and shoulders the blame or responsibility.

Placing responsibility fairly also means that one holds one's child responsible when they have done something to harm or hurt someone else, even if verbally.

My house is part of a larger hospital compound owned by my parents and the hospital staff are as much a part of our household as my cook and driver. There have been instances when Imaad has had an argument with someone in the staff and has said something nasty. I have sat him down until his anger abated and helped him apologize and make up.

Using our privilege to turn a blind eye to behaviour that might hurt someone who works for you is not okay in my opinion. It gives an indirect message to kids that they can vent their spleen on those who are economically weaker than they are and in no position to retaliate. How children treat the domestic staff is a direct reflection on the parent. While a luxurious lifestyle and a life of privilege can dull the child's empathy to some extent, it cannot wholly diminish your influence. I see far too many children talk to the domestic staff in tones that border on the churlish and aggressive, a thing that I cannot condone. A younger person in a position of authority can easily bully and name-call someone if it is passed off with impunity. Please hold your children responsible for their actions too. Not in a shaming and degrading way, but in a way that teaches them that it is important to be respectful and humble.

Teaching your children to practise standing up for themselves

There's a beautiful passage in Nora Bateson's book, *Small Arcs of Larger Circles—Framing Through Other Patterns*, where she shares a bullying episode that happened with her child. Every day on his way to school, her son would be stopped by another kid who would wipe dog poop on her son's clothes. This went on for some time, until Nora decided to help her son practise an appropriate response to the other child's aggression. She taught her son to stand up straight, square his shoulders, look the bully straight in the eye and say no. After practising this over a weekend, her son returned to school on Monday. As soon as he saw the other child, he remembered the weekend training to communicate with body language. Something within him had changed so much with the deliberate and conscious practice that the other child simply walked away.

We may use words and reasoning to tell our children how to be or not to be, but there's something about practising movements, a tone, a sentence, a posture used to communicate an intention, that we become it. One of Imaad's subject teachers in class six walloped him on the head with a notebook or her hand every time she looked at his handwriting. I complained to the school, with no effect. It was a daily dose of humiliation for Imaad and he began to hate the subject she taught. I asked him to practise holding the notebook or her hand firmly, to look her straight in the eye and say, 'Teachers are not supposed to hit students.'

We practised this over two days and the next time it happened, Imu held her hand mid-thwack, looked her in the eyes and delivered the practised statement with a few additions of his own. He was labelled 'a student who talks back', but did the teacher ever hit him again? No.

I was told how ill-mannered my child was when I met the teacher next and I answered that with, 'Maybe he is mirroring his class environment. The next time you hit my child, I'll make sure I grab your hand myself.'

Sometimes you have to stand up for your kids like you mean business and not give a fig for flattery and popularity.

We can teach our children to stand tall. That kind of body language exudes self confidence and can help stave off bullies.

Recognizing ways of relating as not necessarily symptomatic of violent behaviour

Something happens to boys when they reach adolescence and teenage. Some of them transform from these soft, gentle creatures to loud, gesturing beings with a propensity to thoughts of smashing heads, boxing ears and even killing while talking to each other. At least that is what happened to mine. Imaad was never really a very shy kid. He was clingy (to me) as a toddler, but he was naturally protective towards younger kids as he grew older. I remember him carrying extra snacks for a younger child on the bus because this kid cried every day on the ride to school. Imaad would come home to tell me how he dropped him off to class and cheered him up by making paper planes for him. And later, when Imu's cousin Nuhayd arrived, I was surprised by the devotion he showed towards this little boy. He carried him in his arms, didn't begrudge the time that I devoted to the child and shared everything happily. I had imagined that this gentle streak would continue into later in his life.

I wasn't prepared to see Imu change so much into this man-boy who loved yelling over video games with his friends, talking about beating each other up and flying into fits of rage over small issues. I was terrified to see this transformation in him around the age of twelve and it felt like my worst fears about how children of single parents become aggressive would come true. Some of those fears still exist, but over time, I have realized that this change in the attitude of boys towards each other, their bickering and short temper is not always a symptom of an underlying violent streak or serious behavioural issues.

Part of this is discovering ways of expressing and relating to each other fuelled by hormonal energy. Much of it is seen and absorbed via media and observing the older boys teasing and mock bullying each other.

I would get really angry at Imaad for calling his friends names after a fight. I hated the very idea of his turning into a bully. He often reassured me, saying that this was how kids communicated. It didn't mean that they hated each other's guts or meant any harm. That was how boys talked. I recognize this as an offshoot of the toxic culture of competition where name calling and rough handling each other is considered acceptable for boys.

I tried everything from talking about gender norms, making softness and gentleness normal for Imaad from a very early age and this was just so different from what I had thought he'd grow up to be.

It took some of my closest male friends to pacify me and tell me that there's a difference between boys being really malicious and violent with each other and this playful tendency to use slang, tease and bicker. The latter is more a desire to look cool, be accepted in boys' circles and not appear afraid or timid. It doesn't mean that your child will go on a blind killing spree or cause harm to others. My friends reminded me of how loving my child really was: towards animals, children and me. How unafraid he was to show affection, to stand up for friends who needed support or care and how unafraid he was to cry or hug me in public. He had his heart in the right place. The transformation in him was a sign of the age-old ritual to engender camaraderie and instil a sense of belonging.

Of course, I needed to pay attention to how he behaved with girls, how he spoke about and to them; I needed to notice if he was able to feel and show care. When he played his video games, however, it would be okay for him to learn to shoot and even kill.

Over time, I have continued to have serious conversations with Imaad to create a distinction between virtual reality and reality. I keep reminding him that it's important to not stop feeling for others, to not use media as an escape. To which he often tells me that it is an escape. It is a way to live what we cannot live in real life and that every time he goes crazy in a game, he feels like he has let off some steam. 'It's a lot like boxing, Amma,' he says.

I'm not sure if I'm convinced by that argument, but I do feel that it doesn't help to over analyse and overthink everything. I can continue to pay attention without judging my child and calling him violent and aggressive unless I really see his violence and aggression. What I have seen up until now is honestly just a lot of hot air behaviour where these children talk about punching this or that one's lights out; but I see them hanging around each other when they meet. It confuses and annoys me that they have to follow some arcane scripts around masculinity, but I bring my attention to the many lovely ways that my child is off-scripting too and something in me eases up.

Maybe these patterns that we see emerging and changing in our children as they grow, are a call to us to recognize growth patterns that can be generational and cultural. We do need to re-examine our own perspectives and feelings around these patterns to see what can be relinquished to usher in better healing in the way we are as human beings. It is imperative to make peace with the knowledge that we cannot do away with all our existing patterns. I know that it will be hard for me to live like an activist and adopt all the -isms that go with being woke and aware as a parent. I know that if I were to do that, it would also mean that Imaad will be at risk of feeling rejected or isolated in peer groups. I certainly wouldn't want that for my child.

But I do want to practise and live the human qualities of tolerance, care and kindness around him. I do want to remind and lead him to be empathetic and whatever manner or language that manifests in may not always be 'cool' or genteel. As long as I see him embody those qualities when needed, I think I should be okay and not presume the worst.

Creating a counterculture of inclusion

As I've said earlier in this chapter, I think bullying works on the core principle of exclusion; whoever is different or stands out in any way is an easy butt of jokes, comments and even violence. Our children are in as much danger of being at the receiving end of bullying as they are at risk of becoming bullies themselves. When excluding, shaming or beating up someone becomes a sure shot way of gaining acceptance in the strong-boys club or the popular-girls group, it can be very enticing to follow exclusionary trends and join in with the finger-pointing. A sense of belonging is a need that is as ancient as time itself and a lot of us fumble in finding it in healthy ways. For many children, being with the popular kids is the only way they can feel important or valued at school, especially if they don't have the other markers of acceptability at school like good grades. And while we cannot control whom our children befriend, what we can do is create a consistent narrative at home that talks about inclusion and diversity.

What do I mean by that? If your children hear you commenting about a girl's skin tone or body weight or shape, they are more likely to shame others using similar language. If your children hear you praising a child with good grades and calling a child with average grades 'lazy' or 'dumb', they are more likely to pick up on these adjectives and use the same criteria for judging other children. If you displayed prejudice around issues of race, culture, religion and caste, it is likely that your children will pick up on the same cues and react to people who embody any cultural, social, religious, physical or economic difference.

Think of the number of times you heard words and phrases like *moti, kaali, sookha, aalsi, maela kuchaela, bhangi, langdi, kaani, nikkamma, neechi jaat ke, arrey ye to southey hai, Kashmiri saare chor hoten hain, Gujaratis are so kanjoos, kaale log* (fatso, darky, lazy, dirty, sweeper, lame, cross eyed, useless, lower caste, south Indian, all Kashmiris are thieves, Gujaratis are so stingy, black people), in or around your home, in your family and amidst relatives and in gatherings.

The chances are these ways of naming people, children and entire communities is something you might have witnessed growing up. We don't necessarily understand a lot of things when we are little, but they do influence the ways in which we relate to others, especially those others who might be very different from us in their choices, lifestyles and appearance.

I grew up in a conventional Muslim household with very strict strictures about what was acceptable in terms of religion. Homosexuality was considered sinful, and we were told to stay away from 'those kind of people' when we left for college. Now I landed in a college known for its progressive outlook where debates on gender and sexuality were very vocal. No one minced words when it came to these issues. Imagine my shock when I found myself around folks who were openly gay. I didn't really know how to be around them. The voices in my head that belonged to my culture and family kept telling me I should not be friends with 'these people'. But my eyes and body that perceived their warmth and friendliness told me that they were human, like me. Their sexual orientation was not contagious, harmful or sinful. It took me a while to unlearn a whole lot of things I had grown up listening to. Smoking, drinking and drugs were other things I struggled with because they were so alien to me. I did judge a lot of people on the basis of their indulgences in the beginning. Over time, I understood that human nature is too complex for us to use these markers as yardsticks of a 'good' human being. And college did a great job of teaching me to question every idea that had been handed down to me through culture and family.

But most people don't have the privilege of an elite college, good books and exposure to communities other than their own for them to realize that differences in the way human beings look, act, eat and behave are merely superficial.

But what they do have is you who can teach them through example that difference is nothing to be afraid or ashamed of. You can teach them that the discomfort we feel when we come across people who are different from us in any way can be made into a powerful, two-pronged tool—curiosity and empathy. I sincerely believe that these two qualities can redeem us from so many ills. Curiosity turns everything and everyone different from us into someone worth knowing better, someone who is worthy of consideration. When I say curiosity, I do not mean the voyeuristic tendency to gape and point fingers, but a desire to enquire why people do the things they do and how they do them. That alone brings us closer to anyone we see as a stranger. And when we are closer to answers through conversations, reading and questioning, we are that much closer to understanding and empathy.

When our children see us mingle with folks of different communities, regions, religions, sexual orientations, abilities or the lack of them, they become more accepting of differences and less prejudiced or biased. The fear of difference is the engine that has driven the machinery of hate in human history. From witch hunts to the crusades to slavery to colonization to the holocaust to Partition and the current political climate that borders on religious supremacy, difference is the element that has fuelled hatred along with the pulls of power, money and greed. When we are afraid, we kill, attack, shame, label and exclude. Children do the same through bullying.

So, invite differences into your homes as all-inclusive birthday parties and gatherings; as books, stories and movies that celebrate inclusion and diversity. Stay away from shaming language that casually sexualizes choices by calling relationships *chakkars* (affairs) and labelling girls who make choices for themselves 'fast' or 'slutty'. Talk about the many kinds of faiths, sexual orientations and families that exist and that they are just as human as us. All of this might also push you to undo some of your own inherent biases and that can be very difficult. Challenging age-old beliefs that have been intravenously transferred as cultural knowledge and hardwired into one's DNA is hard to let go of. But it's not impossible. I catch myself using words like *motu* (fatso) a lot and I know that even if the context is loving or teasing, it can convey the message that fat-shaming is okay. I'm fat myself and come to think of it, I remember feeling very hurt when someone tells me I was putting on weight or becoming round. I apologize in front of my boy when I slip up and I think that is one way we can normalize messing up, learning, unlearning and relearning. Say sorry, be mindful of your p's and q's and pay attention to what comes out of your mouth.

Pay attention to what your children say about others, how they address visible and subtle differences in others, because they are surely paying attention to you. In a world that is increasingly violent and intolerant, it is hard to imagine that our efforts will make our kids more accepting of other kids and less prone to bullying. But it's a hope we have to keep alive.

Accepting that there's only so much we can do

I am reminded of a yearly *Moharram* (First month in the Islamic calendar, also known as the month of mourning) ritual that Imaad and I used to share when he was little.

Tucked in bed, Imaad would ask me to narrate the story of Moharram since he was four or five. Back then I was married in a Shia household and Moharram was replete with obvious signs and symbols we clung to. We congregated in various *majaalis* (religious gatherings), we didn't wear jewellery, we wore sombre colours. We went to all the neighbourhood *ashras* (ten-day religious gatherings) in the month of Moharram, with little Imaad in tow, his tiny backpack on his back, filled with drawing sheets and colours, at least two toys and a snack. I was apprehensive about taking a toddler to any such gathering where a fussy toddler would be frowned upon. Thankfully mine remained absorbed in his backpack, as long as Amma's *godi* (lap) was at hand. When I left my marital home in 2013, a lot of the shared rituals of Moharram fell away.

While the grief of separation was still fresh, I avoided majaalis, I avoided the family and friends I shared in common with my ex-husband. Gradually I drifted away from even outward practices associated with Moharram like subdued dressing, no jewellery, no celebrations. Perhaps it was my way of shedding an identity I never really identified with—that of a conservative, people-pleasing, Shia wife and *bahu* (daughter-in-law). It was an ideal that broke with my faith and heart. And then I healed, but differently. I wasn't the same person any more.

As I shed everything that I felt I had been doing only to please my family, it was as if the story of Karbala had turned inward and seeped into my being. Freed of all the trappings of keeping up appearances, I began to sift and sieve the narrative for kernels of truth that could be retained in private, as memorabilia. With time, I have found them— the kindness of Imam Hussain and his perseverance to maintain peace; his willingness to forgive, and his immense courage in the face of brutal death; the innocence of Sakina, her ability to dream, love and imagine despite pain; the quiet fortitude of Umm Salima and Umm Kulsoom; the youthful bravery of Ali Akbar and Qasim; the quiet sacrifices of the young women in the camp who relinquished their dreams in light of a greater need; the yearning and pain of Sughra who bade an entire family goodbye, not knowing whether she will ever see them again, and surviving the carnage leading to her final acceptance of grief. Over time, the grace and resilience of Bibi Zainab became a personal lesson for me. All the martyrs and survivors of Karbala from fourteen hundred years ago became inspirations for me, different threads of their stories woven into mine.

One year, around *Ashura* (tenth day of Moharram when the battle of Karbala happened), when Imaad was about ten years or so, we snuggled up at night to talk about Karbala. Every year, as the story is recalled, his understanding of the story's many layers grows in some way as he relates it to whatever is happening in his own life. That year had been difficult for both of us. Imaad had been bullied in school constantly. Despite repeated efforts by both the staff and me, it was difficult to resolve this issue. Imaad's teachers expected him to studiedly ignore the bullies. But the months of forbearance and patience had taken their toll. He was becoming angry and rebellious, and very quick to take offence.

When I finished the story that night, Imaad said, 'I know our lives are insignificant compared to the Imam's struggle, but I think I understand what he did. He tried to negotiate peace with a bully. He offered ways to subdue the conflict, but in the end when it didn't work and he was compelled to defend himself against the forces that wanted to crush his spirit. The boys at school who call me "*naali ka keeda*" (worm of the gutter) and "Pakistani", want to crush both my spirit and my strength. I have tried to reason with them. I have tried to make friends with them. I've complained to my teachers and you have sought help for me, but nothing works. I know what I have to do now. I meant them no harm, and yet they have hurt me so much. Now I will defend myself. It hurts too much, and this is just not right.'

I cannot say if his understanding of Karbala is accurate or flawed. That is his journey; he needs to make it. All I can do is watch and be there when he needs me. I'm just grateful that he's listening to the great ones and learning to love their sorrow. That for me is the essence of Moharram, even if we don't wear black and sing dirges anymore.

Part of the journey of being a parent for me has been to acknowledge that in the larger scheme of things, there is very little I can do. It has made me very accepting of my miniscule existence. It has also made me deeply humble. Some part of coming to terms with the fact that there is very little we can do around bullying episodes will also mean that we begin to trust. Trust in the fact that whatever has passed through you to your child, by means of stories, by means of setting an example to him by your own behaviour, has found its way into the very being of your child. And whatever has taken root within your child will germinate and arise when it is needed. Your child will know what to do when he or she is called to it.

Internalizing this truth has also helped me to not interfere too much in how and in what ways my son grows, and will continue to grow, long after I am gone. I know now that I cannot control everything. I can go to the principal and complain, I can teach my child to project self-confidence, to carry himself with dignity, with strength and offer suggestions for counselling in schools. Beyond that, what can I do? I can't restrain my son from fighting when needed. How much can I tell him to walk away in a world that makes it very hard for those who do? Can I ban him from everything? Can I seclude him or choose his friends for him? Can I monitor everything he watches and reads? I can do some of these at best, but not all.

So even when I disagree with violence, and do not like it when people—even children—fight, there will be times when Imaad will be called to defend himself with his fists, and there is very little I can do about it. I can only learn to be patient and make sure that he is safe. He himself will be the best judge of what he has been called to do, what he can offer, what he can resist or choose to do.

In that sense, this is an invitation for you to know that you can only prepare the soil of your child's being, but how that being develops and what kind of a plant grows from it and bears fruit, depends on a thousand different factors. That depends on the sun, the moon and the stars, the air, rain and nutrition that the soil receives, and all of this is above and beyond you.

Your job is to simply keep ploughing; ploughing and tilling that is done *before* the plant starts growing. After it starts growing, all that is left to do is to prune, water and nourish the tender shoot and pray for good weather.

Chapter 6

Relationships, Love and Dating

I have been called an incurable romantic most of my life. I have mooned over pretty boys, bad boys, sad boys, poetic boys, for as long as I can remember. Now I moon over gorgeous women too. All of this sighing and singing, for more than twenty-five years of my life, made my life beautiful in many ways and painful in some. My family feels that I have wasted much time recovering from heartbreaks and that my progress has been derailed. I agree and disagree.

Maybe my economic progress was slowed due to the many emotional entanglements I managed to get myself into, but my work as a life coach, as an intimacy and couples' therapist has only grown richer through the many meanderings my heart has lost itself on. I can't say it has all been pleasant. Some of it was plain nasty but, hey, I get to take all of that masala to my podcast, my social-media shows and interviews. In the long run, I can safely say that it was a fair bargain. I lost some,

I gained a lot. And at thirty-nine, I'm as ready to fall in love as I was at seventeen, but perhaps a little more safely. We'll explore how to do that in the next chapter on single parents and dating.

For now, it is safe to say that my addiction to romance led me to create (awful and not-so-awful) poetry; it has helped me keep my hope alive and my heart open to possibilities. It has led to my discovering and rediscovering myself sexually and emotionally. It has preserved me from becoming cynical and morose; and that is hard to do after what folks may call a failed marriage and several relationships that did not conclude on the high of a second marriage. Hurting and hoping again takes immense courage and a conscious capacity for regeneration. I feel like this way of being has perhaps taught me to pass on a gentler way of perceiving relationships to my son. It has helped me look objectively at the multiple reasons for a relationship to not culminate in something bigger. And has also safeguarded me from anger, bitterness and blame. And I feel like that is a great perspective on love; one we can surely try and pass on to our offspring.

I know now that placing blame on one person alone for something is too easy and often inaccurate. Life is more complex than that. We cannot expect to bite into a fleshy mango and not have to deal with the stone, much like we cannot hope to raise a child without cleaning its poop and vomit. As my teacher once said to me, 'It is not possible to know anything or anyone intimately without pain.' And I feel like we can learn to do that without despair, without bitterness. And maybe even as we learn to do that and demonstrate that for the benefit of our children, they can perform relationships with less pain to self and others.

For the longest time, my siblings and I didn't know that our parents had chosen each other in college. I don't remember any conversation or teasing about their romance in medical school when we were young, at least not directly from them. As we grew older, we'd hear whispers from *khaalas* (maternal aunts) and *chaachas* (paternal uncles) about how our grandfather, my Nana, had been deeply unhappy about my parents' choice and that he had given in very grudgingly to their *nikaah* (marriage). The sense that we got as we listened to these snippets was that somehow there was something deeply shameful about the whole thing and it couldn't be shared openly. I would notice my mother become stiff around these conversations and my father would remain mostly silent.

When we were in our teens, my parents' marriage hit a very rough patch around their twenty-fifth wedding anniversary and a whole lot of skeletons tumbled out of the closet. We had approached one of our khaalas to intervene and the teenage geniuses that we were, we didn't realize the damage that would do. In the many arguments and conversations that followed, our parents' choice was referred to as a mistake of their youth and my mother would keep referring to marrying my father as a 'sacrifice' she made to make my father happy. I can only imagine what that must've done to my father. It's so sad that she didn't have the freedom to admit that she had married for love.

The sense of the whole episode was one of winning or losing. That somehow my Nana had lost control of his daughter and she ended up making a mistake by marrying my father. My father spoke about his involvement with my mother as a misguided folly. That he was so swept away by her beauty and intelligence that he wasn't thinking straight. Listening to all this left us feeling like our parents' marriage was an accident and we were collateral damage. As I write this, I keep thinking about the unfairness of four young kids having to play referees between their parents. I also think about how it was okay to discuss marital problems in the presence of one's children and yet never okay to talk about the beginnings of love, between them and in general.

The fact that my parents are still married is another story altogether. But in all our years we have hardly heard them speak about love and relationships as natural or joyful. We have never heard them share stories of who eyed whom first, where they first met and talked to each other, what the early days of their relationship were like. None of this ever came up in the context of joy. The overarching tone of their relationship story is sombre.

The only joy we have experienced second-hand from their early years together is through my father's best friend. He shares the events around their marriage and courtship every year on their anniversary. That is the only time we see coyness come alive in our mother and our father nods his head as we gasp and exclaim at his romantic bravado from fifty years ago. And yet there's something that we have imbibed through this all; that love is sacrifice, that when remembered, it invokes more sadness than joy and also that it needs to be hidden. It is only allowed out of the closet after long monsoons to air out any staleness. It can be talked about only when things are wrong.

Of course, a lot of this particular way of experiencing and transferring stories around romance has to do with the fact that our parents were made to suffer for their choice. It is also true that their generation did not have the freedom to discuss their feelings or romantic interests with their elders. Those choices were meant to be made by others. That hasn't changed for a lot of people even to this day. But the way we heard about relationships also has a lot to do with the fact that the overarching cultural narrative around romance has been of shame and secrecy. That is why relationships are perceived as *chakkars* (secret liaisons) that are never approved of by parents. And growing children find it highly entertaining to snoop into flirtations, dating and romantic affairs. Mostly because there is no other way to experience the thrill of romance first-hand in our straitlaced communities. With so much shame and secrecy associated around something, it becomes the forbidden fruit; all the more attractive for its being out of reach.

Love is a grand narrative that is acceptable only if it ends in marriage; attraction is bad and leads to disaster and talking to the opposite sex outside of classrooms is sure-shot evidence of impending doom. This heady mix creates a larger-than-life portrayal of romance and love. And children, especially teenagers, like drama, they like larger-than-life and forbidden fruit. Plus, their hormones don't make it any easier for them to ignore the enticement of the so-called serpent.

I sometimes wonder how our children, or we ourselves, for that matter would be around the opposite gender, or even around each other, if attraction was considered natural and mundane. If there were no hushed whispers or shame around adolescent relationships, I wonder whether even adolescents would look for ways to establish clandestine meetings and a relationship with someone. If romance didn't have to be kept under wraps, I wonder whether our youth would be better prepared and better able to protect themselves emotionally.

Perhaps that openness would also mean that they would be able to share hurt or disappointment and not need to suffer alone.

When we suffer alone, in fear and shame, that feeling grows out of proportion in our minds. Like a secret kept from your friends, the thing germinates into something bigger and weirder because of all the mystery around it. All sorts of rumours circulate around it. So, a shiny new pen can become a dagger and a secret love letter can become a full-blown affair.

I wonder if it would help to create a healthy and wholesome environment for youngsters to experience romance and dating as they grow up, creating an atmosphere of normalcy around discussing matters of the heart. I know that it has helped us.

Demystifying romantic relationships, attraction and dating

When Imaad was in grade five, he had a friend, A. She was feisty, smart and an athlete. Imu and A enjoyed hanging out. Towards the end of the school year, around Imaad's birthday, A came to visit Imu with her mum. I remember opening the door and calling out for Imu, who was upstairs. Imaad dashed down the stairs, ran past A and us and sprinted straight into his room. He emerged a minute later, redolent of the deodorant his dad had gifted him. It dawned on me that my son was experiencing attraction towards girls. My instinct was to tease him about his rushing off to spray himself with perfume before saying hello to his friend, but I knew that my drawing attention to this would only make him aware of what he was feeling and I would only embarrass him.

I remember this time when my younger sister was around ten and she became very close to one of our cousins, B. Now in Muslim families, cousins are not necessarily considered brothers and sisters. They are close, but with the prevalence of intermarriage within Muslim families, young adults consider each other as potential partners. This introduces an element of shyness in their awareness of each other. So B and my sister, Sadaf, were very close. They hung out together, listened to music sharing Walkman earphones; they would take long walks together and play scrabble on long summer afternoons.

In retrospect, I feel that it was completely normal for the two adolescents to form a deep friendship bordering on attraction. But the rest of the extended family started making snide comments about their growing fondness for each other. One of my aunts called them *chidiya* and *chidda* making a *ghosla* together which translates into nesting birds. Someone else would say 'Oh look, they're going to marry each other when they grow up!'

Needless to say, both were acutely embarrassed, and I remember my sister complaining to my mother and asking her to tell people to stop teasing her. My mother just laughed it off, adding, 'It's okay; you can marry B when you grow up.'

I'm not saying that saying this was wrong or right, but comments like this changed the adolescent friendship into something it was not. Both Sadaf and B became very self-conscious and secretive; what was a sweet and innocent friendship changed completely.

I am not disregarding their feelings at the time, but I do feel that when young adults are made to feel like there is no question of a platonic friendship between opposite sexes, it makes their relationship feel uncomfortable and strange. When attraction towards someone is a sign of romance or coupling, or when there are insinuations of marriage, the basic feeling they have towards each other changes. What can be a time of harmless exploration and expression can often become very serious before the kids themselves are ready for it. It's like predicting a storm when the weather forecast says only light showers and a breeze today.

Growing up, we saw this pattern repeat with other cousins and my sisters and I got into quite a few awkward (and painful) situations because there was this hullabaloo around friendships with boys. The same pattern emerged even in school when two girls or two boys became very close. The teachers would pass nasty comments and deliberately separate the two, making the children feel self-conscious and awkward. It was like a spotlight followed them around and all their interactions were broadcast on the daily news. I do think that this unnecessary emphasis on who was talking to whom and 'Oh look, they're sitting together again!' didn't make the already difficult negotiation of adolescence any easier.

Therefore, when I became a mum and when Imaad became an adolescent, I was mindful to not repeat the old paradigms of calling unnecessary attention to relationships and special friendships. I wanted him to feel like his interactions with his friends, both male and female, were perfectly normal. I wanted him to not feel hunted around me. So, I never used phrases like 'Is that your girlfriend?' if he was friendly with a girl. If anyone teased him about a friend saying 'Oh look, that's Imu's future wife!' I would politely tell them to let friends be friends. If they didn't heed this, I did not hesitate to drop my politeness. I was very clear about how I wanted my parents to talk about relationships around my kid as we spent most of our time with them.

There have been times when the school teachers have whispered conspiratorially to me about a budding friendship between my son and a girl in his class, as if it were something shameful. I have always called them out, saying that it was perfectly normal for children to bond, irrespective of gender. There was this one time when a neighbour complained to me, saying that her daughter and my son were hanging out a lot and that it wasn't good. I knew that the children had a huge crush on each other, but I didn't want to blazon it abroad.

I reassured my neighbour that this was only natural and that the more we interfered or shamed their fondness for each other, in a fit of teenage rebellion, the situation would only snowball and get blown out of proportion.

The balanced and mature attitude of the grown-ups help the children deal with broken hearts. In my experience, it has made crushes and adolescent breakups easier to navigate with my child.

The other thing this attitude has made possible is the openness of the communication lines between my son and me. I was the first one to know when he liked a girl at the beginning of this year. I was careful to not scoff at his feelings, but I didn't make a big deal out of it either. When COVID-19 happened, the two lost touch and Imaad seemed depressed for a while. I didn't badger him to just get over it. At this age, the emotional upheavals make adolescents feel extra sensitive and vulnerable; it helps to neither minimize nor exaggerate them. Kids feel safer coming to you with their thoughts and share without fear of shame or judgement. Treating young adult relationships normally also meant that I watched shows like *Atypical* and *Sex Education* with Imaad where we could discuss teen relationships and share insights on healthy behaviour and boundaries.

Some would argue that such TV serials are too advanced, or not age-appropriate for teenagers but I feel that they are already exposed to a lot more through social media. The fact that they're all connected to each other with mobile phones and are online on the Internet, makes it all the easier for them to interact. I feel that media is a great way to initiate conversations around safety in relationships, consent and boundaries, to make relationships feel healthy and natural for our children. I would rather be open to watching shows and reels, sharing and answering questions on anything around relationships with my child than have him go to his peers or take advice from online quizzes on whom to date and whom not to date.

Imaad is nearly fourteen and we often talk about when it will be safe for him to date and the activities with any special friends that I would be okay with. Movies and play dates are completely okay but we have ground rules in place—keep doors open during visits and no texting or talking late at night. We have agreed on random phone checks and unlocked apps on the phone to build trust and transparency. Part of this has meant routinely working on my own biases, limitations and awkwardness. I feel that it is important for parents to address their own discomfort around sharing openly and see where this comes from. Most of the time, it is our own conditioning or the fear that if we normalize attraction and relationships, our kids will start early.

The truth is, folks, your children will start experiencing these emotional upheavals and sentiments around teenage whether you like it or not. By making yourself approachable and supportive, you ensure the child's safety and they don't feel the need to resort to subterfuge or hide things from you.

One of my close friends still bemoans how an innocent, phone-friendship was gaslit by her parents and they forced her into an arranged marriage at the tender age of twenty. She was too young to realize that this need not be the natural outcome of a romantic relationship on the phone. After suffering severe abuse in her marital home, she ended up running away a year later. The fact that our parents, and the generations before them, married early, does not make it okay for us to coerce our children in the same direction. Life has changed so much over the last twenty, thirty, forty, fifty years that generational, social and economic patterns have shifted, changing relationship paradigms as well. And that is okay.

Part of the way one can harmonize these conversations is to be as upfront as possible about one's own experiences. I have frankly answered even the most awkward questions that Imaad has asked me about when and how I met his father, where we went on our dates and what it had been like. Of course, one kept the intimate details to a minimum, but I feel it would have been stupid to lie to him and say we had a conventional arranged marriage. Why should I not share the joy and happiness of my early years with his father, even though it didn't last forever? More than anything, my experience of marriage has made it possible for me to share with him that it's probably not a great idea for everyone to marry young; that I feel it is important to study, work and pursue one's career and hobbies, and then get married only when one is somewhat aware of oneself and not because marriage should automatically follow love.

And I have been careful to not narrate my personal experiences to Imaad in a way that places the blame entirely on his father or any other man I have dated and later broken up with. Talking about situations and differences in opinions and personalities while relating breakups makes it easier for the child to not develop blame-game tendencies. A lot becomes clearer to children with time and there may be some unpleasant facts for them to discover on their own later. Do we really have to talk about relationships ending in a way that makes it look tragic or adversarial? I don't think so.

Some of my friends feel I share too much with Imaad. I see it as preparing a child in a unique situation for the ups and downs of life. The fact that Imaad has not known a stable model of marriage and family life might mean that he will try to replicate marriage and relationships early as a way of healing or feeling completeness. Children from single-parent families do experience the dearth of love and affection growing up, especially when one parent is absent emotionally. They might become more vulnerable to seeking love elsewhere early in life and while that's not a bad thing, one can always try and support kids in a way that they choose out of want and not lack. I will write about this in detail in the chapter on divorce and separation.

Not talking about dating or relationships as a solution to anything

2020 was bad, but 2021 surpassed all nightmarish levels of bad. With the second year in a row during which our children were stuck indoors following the second wave of COVID-19, the possibilities of how to keep them occupied or even functional began shrinking. My child turned into this zombie who had no sense of day or night, playing video games and sleeping at odd hours. The only source of interaction for him was with his friends online and the vastness of the online multiverse. I cannot say that I did a great job at keeping him distracted. But in the face of something that resembled a total systems collapse, what could one lone person do?

There was this sense of acute loneliness in that period. I talked about it with my friends and with Imu too. I noticed a lot of ex-crushes checking up on me and asking if we could make plans to meet after the coronavirus nightmare was over. I remember feeling that the fear of death and disease had made everyone so vulnerable that we all needed intimacy of some sort. I sensed that from Imaad too who was online a lot, talking to his friends (both male and female).

As someone who has looked upon relationships as essential to survival, the idea that I myself needed someone now, more than ever, was very appealing. However, I held myself in check because I was fully aware that we tend to overlook many things when we consider relationships, intimacy and romance as a solution to something. There is no judgement here to say that it is wrong to want love or romance. These are essential to experiencing joy in our lives, but I do want to stay away from the narrative that only these can help fulfil us.

So, when Imu grew particularly close to this one girl when he was thirteen and seemed to spend a lot of time interacting with her, often neglecting his own interests, I knew it was time for me to gently nudge him back to what else could he do to make himself feel happy or busy. This was hard to do. At no point did I want to give him a feeling that he should be ashamed of his interactions or that they were a bad thing, but I did want him to experience himself in more than one context. I would spend more time with him in the evenings playing scrabble or watching movies. At every opportunity, I squeezed in a conversation about making the time to take up projects and hobbies that helped one relax on one's own. This seemed to help him and he began to focus more on developing himself by giving more time to sports.

I cannot say how much this will help, or not help, in the future as he grows older. At nearly fifteen, he still gets very carried away with a crush and has to be reminded to not let his hobbies and passions suffer. The best I can do is model the behaviour I want my son to develop. Over time I have become conscious of taking up activities that help my development. In 2021 I signed up for classes on random things I have been interested in—watercolour painting, yin yoga, Zumba. I try and do something apart from my daily routine and work to show him how important that is. And children watch and learn from us. Every now and then he remembers to take out his sketchbook and draws aeroplanes and zombies. I took him to a football class, and we stood at the side-lines and watched for three evenings until he said he wanted to join too. The COVID-19 year has disrupted our regular schedules and has left us all with so much time on our hands that we are plagued by boredom and loneliness. Young people are isolated and unhappy. With access to other people so easy on social media, extending online relationships or becoming consumed by them is all too easy. But that doesn't really offer a solution to our inner turmoil.

We can talk about relationships in the way children see them—as something one invests in when one likes the person—and not as something to alleviate depression or combat loneliness. Furthermore, we can set an example to our children and demonstrate by our own behaviour the various ways and means by which one can stay occupied and generate joy on one's own and appreciate solitude. I have actively shut down folk who have talked about marriage as a solution to problems.

We've all grown up hearing things like 'Everything will improve once you get married.' I am yet to see anything, or anyone, being 'fixed' by either marriage or children. On the contrary, marriage or breeding used as stopgap measures to 'fix' anything only increases the misery.

Paying attention to what stories we share around romantic relationships and how central we make these to our individual growth and happiness is important. Romantic love is important and it helps us to grow immensely. But it is not an end in itself and I don't think it should be celebrated more than other important relationships—like friendships—in our lives. What we choose for ourselves models what our children are more likely to imbibe. If we celebrate all the important relationships in our lives and keep building skills that enhance other aspects of our personalities, it is likely that our children will learn to do the same.

Dating or relationships can be separate from marriage

Now, after my divorce, when I reflect back on the reasons for my early marriage, I realize that growing up, I had never heard of romance or love acceptable outside of the context of marriage. As soon as anyone discovered that a boy or a girl liked someone, the question of marriage was lobbed at them. There was no concept of exploration and getting to know both one's own self and the other person. The fact that we liked someone or loved someone could only gain legitimacy when we declared that it was our intention to marry that person.

In this context, desire in teenage bodies is the next casualty. Most of the attraction young adults feel is based on the way their bodies are changing and the way they're experiencing themselves and others as physical beings. Girls who had just been girls until a year or two ago, become these mysterious creatures for boys because they look so different. Everything that created a sense of sameness in boys and girls is gone. They look different, they often behave differently and they're even choosing different interests. It's the difference which is attractive.

When I look back at my own life, I wonder whether I would have really married at the age of twenty-one if I had heard desire discussed as something natural around me in my family. Would I have associated desire and attraction with a serious commitment like marriage if I had been encouraged to engage in relationships before a serios commitment? Would I have chosen the first man I felt something for in my body, before I met any others? If I had been told that it was okay to have feelings and marriage could wait, would I have seriously considered my first boyfriend as my future husband? What if I had heard that it was okay to go play the field and know someone, but that twenty-one was way too young to make life-altering decisions?

In the circus that surrounded my marriage, there was only one person, my father's best friend, who asked me to wait one more year after my graduation before marrying.

'The world is very big Sara,' he said. 'You don't know who you are yet.'

Amid the din, when my mental breakdown and suicide attempt made marriage look like a good thing to both me and my family—like a cure almost—no one said anything. In fact, my own tremors fell silent when I saw how excited my mother was, now that 'Everything would be okay with me'. I too believed that I'd be happy thereafter, because I was marrying for love. How was I supposed to know any better?

Maybe I wouldn't have paid any attention to the people asking me to wait, given my frame of mind at that juncture; but I do know that it was the glorification of clandestine love, as this secret/sacred thing, that had made me so vulnerable to it. I didn't give myself enough time to grow into, or out of, my first romantic entanglement because being in love automatically meant that you should marry that person. Sex was legitimized only by marriage and you needed that sanction to live with and be with someone. I remember the innumerable times I wanted to break up with my ex-husband when we were dating, and I couldn't bring myself to do it because the very idea of love was inextricably interlinked with clichéd aphorisms and platitudes: love is special; you make sacrifices for love; you don't just cut and run; love has to be taken seriously and you stick around even when you're suffering.

What could have been a beautiful, exploratory phase of discovery for young people was abruptly turned into a time of critical decision-making. I don't think we were ready to make those decisions when we didn't know who we were, whom we could meet, where we could be or what the world was like.

Unfortunately, we're still living in the shadow of inherited beliefs and ideas, and yet to form our own sense of life. If love, attraction and early relationships were discussed in an open and natural way, and not treated like they were ticking timebombs that we had to either defuse or hurl into the stratosphere, I feel young people could evolve around each other and into love more gently.

My story is not every young person's story, but I do see similarities in the way young people are often not taught how to value themselves when it comes to relationships. Dating is made out to be such a big deal and such a serious issue that a breakup seems like a sin; and a lot of judgement is heaped around being with or separating from someone. The only acceptable way is when you declare that your intentions are honourable and that you want to marry someone.

This kind of rhetoric has seeped into the general discourse over time. I am happy to see that more kids are demystifying dating and relationships by rebelling and transforming the narratives around sacrifice and loyalty.

But it takes an entire system to change radically for old concepts to be debunked or revised thereby increasing health in relationships. By shedding our own antiquated notions about pre-marital sex, dating and relationships, we can gently nudge our children to be healthier and freer in the way they make their choices about partners and whether they want to explore or choose to marry.

Honouring your child's feelings

When Imaad broke up with his special friend early this year, he refused to come out of his room for days. He wasn't eating well and barely sleeping. I was worried, of course, but there was a part of me that was mildly annoyed.

'Why make such a big deal out of such a small thing? He's acting like he has really been in love. The world hasn't come to an end!' Statements like these flitted in and out of my head. Basically, the part of my brain that believed in its assholic supremacy as a parent had been activated. I had to literally drag myself, kicking and screaming down memory lane, back to when I had my first fall out with a special friend to remember what it had felt like. For a teenager experiencing crushes and heartbreak for the first time, it literally does feel like everything and the sky has fallen and the world had come to an end. Negating that and expecting our children to not feel the full spectrum of their feelings is telling them that what they feel is irrelevant.

More often than not, it is our inability to deal with these sudden shifts in moods and to hold space for our children that makes us rush into criticizing our children. Whatever you do, please find a way to tell your children going through a break up or a falling out, that it's okay to feel whatever they are feeling. It takes trust in the innate resilience of our children to hold on to the hope that they will eventually be okay. Please build that trust. Minimizing their feelings or telling them to hurry up and become okay is only going to make your children hurt even more than they already are. We don't need to fix them right away just because seeing them upset upsets us. Remember, this isn't about us. It's about the phases in our children's lives where the enormity of their experience forces them to slow down or react in certain ways. Our job is to comfort them as best as we can and offer support. We can also ask what will help.

My tendency to offer solutions when Imaad is upset or struggling has backfired often. One day he was raving and ranting about a fight he had with a friend and talking about all the scary things he wanted to do to his friend. I went straight into 'Do this, do that and that's not okay' mode.

And he screamed. 'You never listen to me, Amma! When I am upset, I just need you to hear me out. I'm never going to tell you anything, ever!' Those were his exact words. And he stormed out of the room. It took me a while to understand that children usually just vent in anger. They don't mean half the things they say and my tendency to take everything he says literally and offer solutions was making him feel unheard.

I went to his room, apologized and asked him what he would like me to do when he is very upset. 'Just be with me and let me vent, Amma. I will ask you if I need help or advice. I always do. When I'm angry I just want you to listen, please.'

And as simple as that, children tell you what they need if we can find it in ourselves to get off our high horse and ask them what they would like instead of taking it as an opportunity to force our opinions on them. It takes humility and acknowledgement of the fact that our children are not us and they never will be, to be able to ask them what they need. Our lives, our younger years were not as complex or as full of interactions as our children's. We need to honour that and respect the fact that love, crushes and relationships in young adults are real. They exist.

They may have existed differently in our times.

We may have experienced all this rush of emotion in something as simple as walking someone to and from school, or making eye contact in tuition classes, or at the most, talking on the phone in secret. And that was life-shaping too. But we were just as dramatic as our children. We wrote letters in chicken blood and became Meena Kumari and Devdas when our hearts were broken. We stopped eating and bathing when we discovered that the person, on whom we had a crush, liked someone else. Romance was our whole world back then. A smile, a giggle and a love note could make or break our day, our week; just as a text or a shared meme make our children's days. They have better access and more opportunity and that makes their involvements even deeper in some ways. They share and exchange more, they have more avenues to meet and talk. And, of course, they will feel the rush and pangs of romance. It will help us be kinder and patient to remember and honour that. Above all, it will help our teenagers to navigate relationships with more support and less judgement.

Setting healthy boundaries

It's a tricky dance, holding space for children and making sure they are safe. We cannot negate the reality of their experiences but, as parents, there are certain things I know my child will be better off experiencing later rather than earlier. There's also the question of ideations that I and my family may be openminded and okay with, but the world around us may not be as accepting. Part of our job as parents is to teach our children to navigate this tricky area. We don't exist in isolation as individuals or families. So, I could be completely cool with my teenage son talking to girls or inviting them home, but my larger reality is that I share space with my elderly parents. They are mostly supportive, but their ideas about what is, and isn't okay, are different.

Life cannot be simplified to instructions like 'do this or that'. I wish it were but it isn't. This is where boundaries help. And the easiest, most effective way of setting boundaries is being consistent and open in how you communicate them. For example, every time my son brings up things like dating and having friends over, I use that as an opportunity to gently explain what is possible for us to do and what will not be okay—it's okay for him to go to the movies with friends or go out for a meal on birthdays or after exams; he can have friends over for the evening or the day; but I cannot allow overnight stays or push for them just yet. Maybe when he is older, and the other children's parents are just as willing as I am, it might be possible.

As it looks like my son is heterosexual, my challenges will be around allowing him the freedom to explore interactions with girls while making sure they are both safe and protected. I am yet to find a parent around me who is okay with sending their daughter over to spend the day. And when some of Imu's female friends visit for short periods, I make sure to ask them to keep the doors open. I may be okay with the children having privacy, but I don't want my child to get in trouble later with his friend's parents or for the female friend to feel uncomfortable in any way.

Communicating how you want your child to perceive the opposite sex, or what is, and what isn't, okay to share, is also important to me. I keep an eye on the way Imaad talks about girls and women and we often have chats about inappropriate language. I have been very frank in telling him about the kind of pictures to share or ask for. These are things no one will teach your children. I have been as blunt as to say, 'Please never ask for nudes and don't share yours either.'

If there is some interaction like that, make sure it is not forced and the other person is comfortable and willing. I could shut my mind to the fact that this could ever happen, but who am I kidding? I could 'forbid' this too, but again, who am I really kidding? No amount of 'forbidding' anything has ever worked at any point in time, and it is best if we accept that our children will grow up to experience desire and it will manifest in different ways. We can teach them how to keep themselves and others safe.

Depending on your own priorities and the values or ideas you may want to share with your children when it comes to how they experience relationships, please find ways to have open communication with them.

One thing I have struggled with is helping Imaad understand that families in our neighbourhood, or in his friends, circles, may not be quite as open to discussion or sharing as we are. So, this one time, Imaad had a huge crush on a girl in the colony beside ours and he would inveigle ways to talk to her. She responded and they began meeting to cycle together in the afternoons. One time, Imaad wanted to call her and couldn't get through to her mobile phone. A friend shared her father's telephone number and my young man called the father in all innocence to say he would like to speak to his daughter. The same evening, the gentleman's wife was at my door, telling me how angry her husband had been and that it was 'not good' for children to be so close or talk so much. She also said that her furious husband had taken away the daughter's phone and had given her a severe scolding.

I can't comment on what the right or wrong attitude was for the girl's parents in this scenario. However, I did use this incident as an opportunity to explain the different family dynamics to my son. I could tell him that not everyone is going to be cool about certain things and if he liked a girl, he would have to make sure she didn't get into trouble because of something he did or said. It was also an opportunity for me to explain he had to be careful not to expect the same level of openness from others that he gets from me. Naturally, he didn't like that, but it is true that the world is a strange place and different families have different approaches to what is okay and what isn't. It's best he learns that from me rather than discover them by getting himself into painful situations.

It's still too early to say what works and what won't for our strange little family. Perhaps there is no one way that things work or fail. But it gives me comfort when my child tells me that he feels safe talking to me and feels he can tell me anything. This also means that he asks me anything and teases me no end when he sees me happily chatting on the phone with a man.

It is special, the ease with which we can be ourselves around each other. It is a gift I wish more parents get to experience with their children. But it is a gift that takes conscious nurturing.

Chapter 7

Single Parents and Dating

.

'Amma, do you love Uncle P?' Imaad asked me one day when he was nine. Uncle P was one of my closest friends at that time.

'I love him as we love friends, Imu. He is very dear to me,' I replied.

'No, I mean do you "love" love Uncle P?' he persisted. I wasn't sure what to say. There was definitely more than mere friendship between Uncle P and me (in hindsight, I can say that we were deeply in love with each other), but I was surprised and unsure about how much to tell Imaad. I asked him why he wanted to know this.

He replied, 'Amma, I'm asking because I love Uncle P. I really wouldn't mind if you wanted to marry him. I think we would be happy together, all three of us.'

Despite my child's innocent hope, Uncle P and I never worked out and we parted with a lot of unnecessary bitterness which affected Imaad as well. We were able to resolve some of that bitterness and float back to a place of familiarity and friendship after a year of silence, some awkward conversations, a few non-date dates and some brutal honesty with each other. Most of the work back to friendship was done by Uncle P, to be honest. I was too emotionally shaken to be calm about the whole thing. It is much easier now. We meet once every few months, have a cuppa chai when he's in town or we catch up on the phone. He still makes me laugh a lot.

I learnt a lot from that experience as a thirty-five-year-old single mother trying to find love again. One of the things I learnt was that whenever I felt like I had found or lost love, I wouldn't be the only one finding and losing it. My son would feel it almost as acutely as I did. His yearning for a father figure would probably always make him hope and that hope would bring him as much sadness as it would bring me when the dream faded.

Adults tend to believe that children don't understand things like relationships and romance, that they are too innocent to notice. I feel that it is this intuitive innocence, which is natural in all children, that makes them acutely aware of any changes in relationship structures around them, anything that is new or anything that has ceased to be. And when they feel and know so much, it is important that we talk to them as honestly as possible. Yes, we cannot always treat our children as our friends and confidantes. It is too great a burden to bear for them. But we can ease their worries, answer their questions with appropriate truths and most of all, we can show them how to be graceful in love and loss. And none of this is easy to do. The way we transmit, translate and share our thoughts about relationships pretty much depends on our internal frame of reference.

Although this is not a book for single parents, I believe that the way single parents navigate their relationships and unique challenges in general does have an impact on their children. Perhaps if we consciously monitor ourselves as we ford the crosscurrents of relationships, we will help provide some degree of clarity to our children as they observe and absorb. Single parents often become the locus of their children's lives and by virtue of that, whatever they do is in the full glare of the spotlight. With that in mind, I want to share a few things I have learnt in my nine-year-long career of dating as a single mum.

After a big breakup, divorce or death of a partner, please take time to heal and introspect

For the longest time, my internal frame of reference about relationships was an either/or frame. That if one has a steady romantic relationship, it is everything or nothing, and it can only be good or bad. And by translation that also meant that a life where you had a good relationship was beautiful, perfect and somehow complete. And when that relationship broke or changed, life itself became damaged or derailed. And this frame didn't belong to me alone. It has been passed down to me through family, through popular culture and media where romantic relationships are considered a sign of personal success, as something that makes us who we are. Naturally, one grows up wishing for that kind of love and fulfilment and anything less, like a breakup or a divorce, feels like a personal failure.

Reading about anything is like looking at a picture, any picture, and noticing all the colours and shapes in it; but reading about it is a far cry from actually being in that picture.

If we were to somehow become a part of that picture, we'd experience the heat or cold, the warmth or lack of it on our skin. I would read about self-worth issues around relationships and just see those sentences, those lines without internalizing their full import. Experiencing tremendous pain in my marriage and then going through divorce was like watching a documentary about Antarctica one day, and the very next day, being in that documentary, surrounded by raging blizzards, severely underprepared, freezing cold and feeling the threat of death at every second.

In retrospect, I am glad that by the time Imaad was old enough for me to talk about relationships and dating, enough time had passed for me to process my own pain around my marriage and divorce. The work that I did also allowed me the long-lens vision to look at the other factors that contribute to young people feeling especially vulnerable and at the mercy of their emotions in relationships. Pain in relationships is like seepage in a room where the source of that seepage lies hidden in some obscure pipe embedded deep within the walls of a house. But the damp and rot of it is felt by all the people in the room. It touches the objects, furniture and even clothes with its dank musty smell.

Everything we experience in relationships in our childhood goes on to influence our role or the way we behave in adult relationships. The way we recognize love and relating, the way we express tenderness or anger, how we perceive conflicts and respond or react during them, how we communicate positive and negative feelings in adult relationships—all of this has roots in the primary relationship between our parents or any other close relationships we witnessed in childhood. Some of these relational patterns imbibed in childhood are not necessarily healthy. A lot of families may be used to not addressing conflicts and concerns openly while some may avoid addressing them altogether. In some families, parents may extend love and care only when children display complete obedience to parental desires. Some parents are not expressive at all when it comes to affection or displeasure while others may regularly resort to anger and violence as corrective measures. How we have witnessed our parents perform their roles towards each other and us go on to create a unique sense of how we experience ourselves in a relationship and how we behave.

I grew up in a family where love entailed supreme sacrifice. Love wasn't something you chose for the sheer joy of it but because you had committed to the idea of it. The story of my parents' marriage is not mine to tell—at least not yet. But being a minor character in that story, the idea instilled in me was that one kept at relationships and marriage as long as one was alive, that love requires the relinquishing of one's personal dreams and projects and that the partner, particularly the husband, came first, and the wife needed his protection and care—all of these were like the tag lines of a story in a children's storybook. And this minor character was watching from the sidelines with wide-eyed wonder, silently lapping up this wondrous tale of love.

By the time I was a teenager, the story of love had become the very axis of my being; an axis that was way bigger than I was and bigger than everything else in me. My tastes, my talents (which I thought were none at all at the time) and reality itself, did not matter as much as this idea of love. One could say that this was a natural hijacking of my personality by my teenage hormones. But, as I look back, my hormones continued to hijack my personality well into my thirties. Even now, I have to fish out the tattered remnants of my personality with the help of all the healing techniques and tough-love friends I know and put myself back together when there is heartbreak. It has been difficult to treat love or romance as only a part of me and not all of me so that it doesn't eclipse my work, my child, my family.

I think a large part of my being a hopeless romantic was because I had suffered abuse as a child, which had deeply undermined my sense of self-worth, and I kept looking for approval in relationships. When one grows up with low self-esteem, feeling like a piece of garbage that attracts hurt and disgust, it is hard to love oneself. This is why one tends to seek love and validation from others. We rely on the way we are perceived by others, their compliments and admiration to make us feel good about ourselves, because nothing else does.

And if you add a predilection for romantic poetry and fiction, coupled with the generational stories around love, relationships and marriage, that fictional world becomes one's ideal. It is a potent and magical mix, that dream partner who always remains just beyond our reach. We see reflections of this in so many fairy tales in which a prince in shining armour or the sleeping princess are the solutions to unhappiness who will change our sorrows into joy and create the life of our dreams.

I think I pursued this immutable Disney story until very recently, when heartbreak upon heartbreak compelled me to stop chasing after rainbows and take responsibility for my own joy and growth. It was bloody hard. It was heartbreaking to accept that my marriage wasn't working, that the love I had thought would last forever was making both me and my then husband miserable. It was terribly painful to accept that our childhood traumas had chained us in victim frames where we kept expecting our partner to save us, even at great cost to their own self. I tried to be that saviour, but we cannot save anyone, not even ourselves entirely. It takes an entire system of nurturing and caring to help support an individual.

When I walked out of my marriage, my world felt like it had ended and that is what I kept experiencing through the responses of others:

You live for your son now, forget everything else.

You've already tried this, haven't you? It's now time to care for Imaad.

Don't run after love.

As if love was this one-time harvest that once cut would never flourish again and the land of our being would remain barren forever. It was so hard to go through that and to come alive again to the idea of planting new seeds, hoping for a different crop to grow, to want to smell different flowers, to walk on wet earth again. And maybe this whole notion of love and relationships as a one-time blossoming of our souls made it so hard for me to leave my marriage too. It took me eight years to step out of a relationship that had been hurtful at too many levels to describe. Everything I had known about love was challenged by this desire to run screaming from the relationship. And that prevented me from heeding my own needs for years.

The process of recovery from my divorce through therapy and so much inner work through my Neurolinguistic Programming (NLP) community, my work with my teacher Bhavana Nissima and with my peer group, not to mention the extensive reading I did, gave me a clearer sense of how to separate my need for a partner or love from how functional I could make my life. This also meant that I worked on my trauma and took responsibility for my well-being. I had to free myself from the idea that healing could only happen through the love of a man. The process was and continues to be exacting but it has helped me see clearly; it has helped me look at potential partners not as saviours but as collaborators to life building and happiness. And that has really realigned, reworked and recreated my perspective on relationships and dating. And I couldn't be more grateful because this change in me has coincided with the time in my child's life when he is experiencing attraction, affection and relating in a unique way.

And all of this is important work because what we have imbibed in our own younger years has the power to shape how we demonstrate relationships as parents, especially when we are single parents. Society would have us (especially women) sew up our hearts (and our vaginas) and not seek love or sex after divorce or widowhood. But that's neither healthy nor entirely possible without being utterly miserable. If we are to live, thrive and find companionship after divorces, breakups and partners' deaths without replicating past pain, single parents can create healthier ways of doing so and demonstrating this for their children too. To help us heal, we need to forgive both ourselves and others and rewire some of the unhealthy ways of being in relationships we may have learned as children. In consciously desisting from bequeathing dependence and rancour, we can model graceful 'relationshipping' for our children.

And when we take responsibility for our past by recognizing our part in a bad relationship, we restore a fuller picture of the world. And we pass on that picture to our children. Barring some people who have been in abusive relationships and suffered pain, most relationships are a two-way street. And it is important to remember them as such or we are forever at the risk of blaming the universe for our pain and not doing anything to create joy for ourselves. Even in abusive relationships, some of our own patterns and societal structures make it possible for the abuse to continue. It is important to recognize this so we don't internalize shame and consciously avoid the paths that make us victims. Thereby, as parents, we model taking on responsibility for creating joy in relationships for our children. We are showing them that it is possible to create new ways of relating with the world and with each other.

Dating as a single parent AND keeping our children safe from hurt

My first 'adult' relationship after my divorce was with a very sensible gentleman based in Delhi. I was so taken by the fact that it was possible to have mature, stable interactions with this person that I overlooked the improbability of our getting married or being together long term. There were issues in his family that he couldn't work through to be with me. And being a single parent, I should've probably realized that if I couldn't be with this person on a permanent basis, then it was probably not a great idea to introduce him to my child. But the heart is a greedy thing; it wants more and even more. So, I introduced my son to him. Imaad became deeply attached to him. A few months later, this person and I broke up. He was to marry someone else. It was a horrible time for me. And the fact that somewhere along the line I had exposed my son to the vulnerability of heartbreak made me feel awful and irresponsible.

When one has been hurt in love, which is the case with most single parents, it can be easy to overlook difficulties with or lapses in a new person and it might be an attractive thought to include that person in our mental image of a wholesome family. There is a need to feel fulfilled in that sense and feel complete again. And there's nothing wrong in that. But, more often than not, relationships will not work out for twenty different reasons. And we might be left dealing with our own hurt as well as explaining to our children why we broke up or working to mend the hurt they feel because of the absence of someone who briefly became a part of their lives. We can't always predict who we'll end up being with in the long term or who is suitable for us, but we can wait until we feel fairly sure before we bring a new person into a family dynamic that may already be fragile.

I didn't learn this the easy way.

Long after this incident, I befriended a gentleman who lived in the US, and we began to chat very regularly on the phone. He was a lot older than I was and seemed ready and willing to accept me as a life partner, child and all; and I liked him enough to want to meet up and see where this took us. He insisted that I let him speak to Imaad so he could get to know him too. But something in me said it was too early to bring my son into the picture. I felt we could wait until we were more sure of each other, and not get ahead of ourselves. But, as I said earlier, I was desperately seeking the idea of home and family and was impatient to fill that gap, albeit subconsciously. Looking back, I realize that this void in my life made me impetuous and hasty. Imaad started speaking to him and grew very close to him. I was happy, but also afraid.

As quickly as things had looked up, they crashed. COVID-19 happened and after the lockdowns, it became very clear that this relationship would be difficult to sustain. Instead of talking through the whole thing, this gentleman disappeared. He stopped speaking to either of us. I was hurt but my son felt betrayed. I hated myself for letting this happen. In retrospect, I know that there was little I could have done to foresee this disaster.

Single-parent families are hungry for love and affection in many ways. This is something the 'superhero', single-parent brigade does not want to accept or admit. We may make things work beautifully on the outside, but on the inside, the emotional, psychological and financial responsibility of running things alone make us crave support. That is only human. It makes us include potential partners very easily into our family. That doesn't mean that we stop dating or looking for joy. It's just that perhaps it would be better to keep our children at a safe distance from our romantic relationships until such time the person shows enough potential to become part of the family in whatever way. These things take time to unfold. And it is important we give ourselves that time to know a partner in multiple contexts before bringing our children into the picture. Doing so will keep our children safe from the instability and the ups and downs we go through when we break up or meet someone new.

One way to do that, without negating our need for partnership, is by telling our children that we may date, that we may be going to see someone, but that does not mean that it has to translate into something serious very quickly. I tell Imaad when I am going on a date and even when I don't tell him, he figures it out and it is best that I own up before he asks. But I create a boundary around how much I tell my kid about who, what and where. He doesn't need to know until the person has been in my life for a significant amount of time. Healthy relationships need more than romantic dates to unfold and making that happen takes time. We don't have to share everything with our children about where/with whom/ what until things are more certain or the children are a lot older and can handle things better. This can be difficult in single-parent households where the logistics of babysitting the children when you are out is also important.

Create your village/alibi network

Dating and romance post-divorce would have been impossible for me had it not been for my sisters and my many friends who stepped in at different times to babysit my son so I could experience something I badly needed. It took me time to step out of my conditioned guilt and shame around wanting a relationship and a normal sex life after my divorce. My parents are conservative, and my religious background made it difficult for me to even think about sex outside of marriage. But denying myself that basic need for connection and intimacy was brutal. Working through those mental blocks, I emerged at a place where I was okay about being who I was. I was okay accepting the fact that marriage may be hard to come by and that I wasn't even sure whether I wanted it again. But I did want companionship. And to make that happen, I needed a network that would support me and step in when I needed time away from family.

Our culture and society make it so hard for divorced/ separated and single parents, especially women, to have romantic relationships. There is so much judgement and criticism heaped on us for wanting joy and beauty and for wanting intimacy, that very often we resort to secrecy and subterfuge. It is a very unpleasant feeling to have to lie about feeling something so basic and human. But it is what it is. Over time, I have learnt to reframe secrecy as sacredness—a private space that my parents and my family need not be a part of because they cannot be a part of it without causing hurt to me or themselves. But I do need support. And this is where my community of friends have really helped. I have learnt to ask for help openly. I have learnt to tell them that I need them to step in for me so I can go out. I have learnt to not feel shame when I ask this. I have learned to recognize and be grateful for help and support when it is extended.

These networks have helped me immensely, supported me and stepped in for me also because I have invested in them. I showed up whenever they needed me. I was there to support in whatever way I could when it was needed. Modern language has sullied the word 'transaction'. The origins of it lie in the beauty of human exchange that is neither measurable nor tangible. But it is life-affirming and life-saving. Please find time to create your villages, your communities. As single parents who are made to feel that they exist somewhere on the outer fringes of society, it is vital that we create pockets of belonging so we can feel refreshed and strong. More than the kinsfolk with blood ties who tend to impose their own sense of right or wrong on you, it is these hand-picked families who will hold you up and offer respite.

And as you create this oasis for yourself, please pack away guilt and shame about the fact that you need to do this for yourself. In a world that denies us joy openly, it is okay to be a fugitive and seek it on the sly. I think of this kind of fugitivity as a kind of turtle life; I have an inner universe tucked into my shell and it is for me to enjoy. When I feel safe and ready to be visible, I poke my head out and say hello to the world. I can be both visible and invisible at once. It is okay to want to be something other than mom or dad sometimes. Being that helps us to return to our children with less resentment and more joy. So, call up that friend you trust and drop off your child with them when you want some time for yourself. Or call a friend over to babysit when you want a break. Make friends with other single-parent families so you can step in for each other in times of sickness or travel. And work with your discretion and good sense when you do that. Not everyone will have your set of parenting principles but some things like safety for your children should be non-negotiable. So, it is okay if a particular friend will feed your child noodles two days in a row as long as that friend will also take your kid to the park and read him bedtime stories, give lots of hugs and keep him safe.

Take time to know your own heart

Reaching for a band aid, a salve, a painkiller is natural when we are hurting. Sometimes the business of living does not even allow us time to pay attention to what hurts. Is it a cut? a bruise? or is there a ligament tear beneath that requires attention and time to heal? Most times, getting rid of the pain is all you can think of, especially when you've lost a marriage, a home and multiple relationships. Or when you suddenly find yourself doing things that require a whole village to pull off. There is never enough time to pay attention to our own pain. I get that.

It is also scary to face whatever it is we are running away from—grieving or anger or guilt. Who wants to open that can of worms? We just want to move on to feeling better in any way we can. And for those folks who are suffering the end of marriages or relationships, other relationships, flings, sex is like salve. We want to experience ourselves afresh in relation to someone else, someone new who will make us feel alive or different, who will make us forget the pain of loss. And that's okay. What is not okay is going into this impulsively, without realizing whether this is what we really need or if it's something we're just doing because we finally can.

I've worked with too many people who are emerging from divorces and breakups to not clearly say that consecutive flings and relationships created without having given themselves a sufficient mourning period are coping mechanisms. This is not me trying to put a moralistic spin on casual relationships or sex, but someone who has used relationships herself to dull the pain of grief. There's nothing wrong with that. Except like all coping behaviours, these have lasting destabilizing effects too. And anything that destabilizes and impacts us, will impact our children. And do we want to remain impulsive in our choices or do we want to be conscious of why we do the things we do? And when we answer that question, maybe we can use other, healthier ways of seeking the things we need?

The answer is not in abstinence from sex, dating or relationships, but in creating enough pauses in your life to identify the root of your pain. And to take the time to find courage and feel it fully, to heal oneself enough to see what we really want. And that is not easy. It's messy, dirty and snot-inducing work. But it is worth it in terms of gaining clarity and balance in the choices we make in our quest for love. The burden of our emotional responsibility as single parents is magnified if we add more stresses to our system without taking the time to work through them. That creates more havoc, more pain.

I ask single parents to please take time to know your own heart. To understand and befriend your pain before you seek to drown it in someone else's body. And if, after doing that, you know you want only casual relationships, fine, go ahead and do it. Be happy if that is what gives you peace. But if you know that you seek a deeper connection and love again, then don't settle for anything less. Give yourself time to look for what matters to you. We don't have to be pigeon-holed into a convenient category of how to love simply because it is cool. Nothing about life is convenient. And within that constraint we can find our freedom if we just find it in us to pause and reflect.

In that pausing and reflection we are likely to recognize and embrace ourselves. And as we do that, perhaps we can be freer to embrace our challenging roles as single parents with children who will always need more of us. Our children deserve that.

Chapter 8

Going Through Separation and Divorce

I remember reading somewhere that going through divorce is like experiencing death in the family. You lay a living, breathing relationship to rest. But unlike death, there are no rituals to ease us into the sadness that follows the end of a relationship. There are no public and private ceremonies that honour and release the many stories that make the fabric of a marriage. There is no form of mourning that will allow us to lament the remains of a shattered dream. Divorce, I feel, is a uniquely lonely experience. You are answerable to many and often a subject of curiosity and shame, but hardly ever are you allowed or encouraged to mark the passage of love. And I think this adds to the bitterness and anger that often accompany divorce.

I understood this excruciating truth when I experienced the breaking up of our family and a complete change in our personal circumstances. Both my son and I had to struggle with hurt, confusion, a sense of betrayal and the loss of hope for years until we reached some clarity. There was really no time for me to feel my way through this massive change. The physical realities of fighting the divorce case (something that could have been avoided), of caring for my son alone with no support from my ex-husband or his family, left no room for me to grieve. I was sleepwalking through a nightmare for three years after my separation. It was only after the divorce was finalized after endless arguments, pleadings, court visits and breakdowns that I could take the time to live my pain and my son's pain. The only thing that helped us through that difficult time was holding on to the truth of our situation, to self-respect and a deep commitment to not harbour hate or ill will while actively remembering the past with fondness and gratitude.

Even with all that effort and my every resolve to not be bitter and hurt, I would unravel every time my child would say, 'I miss Abba. I miss him so much.' In those moments, I would be swamped by guilt and wished with all my heart that I could change things for him and give him the emotional stability that others like him have had. Maybe I should have tried harder; I am a bad, selfish parent. Remorse and debilitating self-reproaches like these would cripple my strength and I had to forcibly safeguard myself against them. There was no going back. I would repeat to myself what I have often shared with every parent going through divorce and separation—you did the best you could and as much as was humanly possible. Accept the fact that you cannot change the past, but you can try and make your future better. You can try to divorce with grace and dignity.

This chapter is dedicated to including children in the grieving process that accompanies divorce and the confusion that precedes it. Children have no control over the circumstances that compel their parents to separate and very little understanding of why it needs to be done at all. Imagine the helplessness of a child who has no clue about why he or she must leave home and get used to the absence of one parent. It is frightening to say the least. And the adults involved in the situation are going through such an emotional upheaval themselves that they often overlook comforting and explaining things to their children. In this space, we will need to bring back the focus on creating safety for a child where he feels uprooted, just as the parent feels uprooted. We will need to seek to share as honestly as possible, allowing room for grief, anger and sadness for both the parent and child.

Reframing divorce

Beyond The Last Act
11 April 2016
In an effort to explain your lingering attachment to me
You have cited the decade we spent
Tied to each other
And the child we made together
As reason enough for me to stay
To look beyond your infidelity
My sorrow our common loss
And try once more
What was once can be made again you say
How do I convince you?
That those years together were
Merely a blink in the cosmic
Dance of life

Life that does not heed personal loss
Life that cannot and must not
Cease
Think of us as two dancers
Who enjoyed a temporary embrace that
Was perhaps real
Or perhaps imaginary—
A play put on to satisfy the
Hungry urges of time
We loved we laughed we wept together
And we rested in the shadows waiting
For a new act to begin
Soliloquies and conceits
Displayed in all their madness
But I have heard the curtain call
Straining for a while
Maybe you hear it too
And pretend to ignore it
Let it fall my bygone lover
Fellow dancer
Let us take a bow and hope
That the audience will remember
Only our grace and not
The clumsy way we used to fall

I wrote this poem on the back of a book I was carrying to court six months before my ex-husband agreed to sign the papers. I had seen him that morning, angry and aloof, held tightly together as if wrapped in cellophane. He was sitting beside his lawyer who was trying to tell me what a terrible mistake I was making; leaving a man who had hurt me in every possible way. He kept telling me how the onus of holding the home together fell on the woman, no matter what the man said or did. It wasn't the first time I was hearing such regressive, sexist preaching and it wasn't going to be the last. I nodded and told the lawyer that maybe that's what he would say to his own daughter if she was suffering. I have no doubt that that is exactly what he would do.

I put a hand on my ex-husband's elbow and said to him, '*Jaane do. Ho gaya bohut ye. Rishta khatm hua hai, ham zindagi kyun khatm kar rahen hain*? (Let this go. We have been through enough. Only our relationship has ended, why should stop living because of it?' After years of fighting us, me, our reality, I saw something in him thaw. He nodded slightly and said, '*Dekhten hain. Mujhe thoda* time *do.* (We'll see. Give me some time.)' This was notwithstanding the fact that I had waited patiently and impatiently for more than three years for him to accept the end of our marriage and release us both. And I waited some more. It happened eventually, at the end of that year. It was the beginning of a protracted release of agony that lasted another two years, years in which I finally came to terms with my grief. I am wondering aloud, writing here, what made the journey less bitter for me, less cynical and hypercritical. And I see it clearly now, something I couldn't see even as I wrote the piece that talks about looking at a failing marriage as a passage; a blip in time composed of both joy and sorrow, one that can end and one that is not unnatural in its ending.

What I am referring to is the ability to see and understand divorce as not an end to life or possibility, not a disaster or personal failure and definitely not a blemish on one's character or life story. This did not come naturally to me. I remember feeling like my whole world had collapsed when I made the decision to leave my marital home. I felt like I would never be happy again, that I had failed in every way possible; as a mother, as a wife, as a woman. I remember clinging to the walls of my Aligarh home a few hours before I left and howling like an injured animal. I remember looking at every plant I had watered in the garden and every little household item I had decorated the house with as if it held my life force, my very breath. Everything felt like an absolute amputation, a cleaving of my body in two.

When I look back, I recognize that a lot of that past pain was mine but more than that, it had been passed on to me through culture and society generationally. Marriage is the ultimate mark of normalcy in our culture and a marriage that does not end in divorce, no matter how hollow it is from the inside, is a mark of personal success. It is the gold medal you wear around your neck as a woman who has managed to 'keep her man and her home'. For men it is the stamp of honour that makes them respectable in other people's eyes. He could control and keep his wife, he was the ultimate man. An unbroken home, no matter how full of sadness, rancour and anger, is seen as the perfect bedrock for children. And I had, like many others around me, internalized these stories about marriage and divorce. So, when things became so unbearable that I had to leave, I left feeling like I had committed a grave sin against my son, my family and even my own self, even when that sin released me.

I feel one of the ways that we can make this passage, this necessary separation or divorce easier for us and our children is to revise, rewrite and reframe traditional narratives around divorce and marriage. How can two people, or even one person, choosing their happiness over pain or joy be a failure? Maybe it is a breach of trust, or a fading of love, or an emergence of irreconcilable differences, but I don't think it is a failure. Failure would be holding on to the debris of something that was once beautiful in the deluded hope that it will become whole again. That is failure for me because, by doing that, we prolong the misery for others and ourselves. Failure would be deliberately turning a blind eye to the disaster happening right before our eyes, and wishing that it weren't real. Failure would be remaining ignorant about the deep unhappiness of a spouse or our own unhelpful behaviour that may be causing an irreparable breach in the marriage. But carefully choosing to end something after thought, effort and dialogue is not failure. I think it is honourable and honest.

One of the many reasons we stay on in unhappy relationships and marriages is concern for the well-being of our children. Our cultures tell us that children need both parents, that they need stable homes and not fragmented families. And that is true. But what is also true is that homes don't become stable or safe through marriage or commitment alone. If that were true, children from 'unbroken' homes wouldn't spend so much of their adult lives in therapy, seeking relief from the wounds of their childhood. Here's something I read in Jeff Brown's beautiful book of essays, *Hearticulations* that says this in a much more nuanced way:

> 'I grew up in a broken home. But not because my parents divorced. It was broken long before, when love turned to hate. When they finally divorced, there was actually more room to breathe. All the energy that went into managing the breaks, could be channelled into healing. It's time we re-frame the shaming term 'broken home'. It is riddled with assumption and judgement. And it neglects the fact that many single parents hold their families together beautifully. While many seemingly intact families are deeply broken. Because a home is not broken when parents

separate or divorce. A home is broken when there is an absence of love. If there's love, nothing's broken.'*

If we are to live with ourselves in equanimity and pass on the same to our children, post-divorce or separation, the baggage of guilt and shame that comes with old ideas around divorce needs to go. And internally reframing our experience of this can create powerful shifts in how we handle divorce or separation. If we keep looking at the loss of a partner through divorce as an attack on our manhood or a failure of our womanhood, we will remain mired in blame and continue to struggle instead of accepting and moving on. And the more we do that, the less our children will have a chance to re-imagine and reshape their future post-split. What parents carry as failure is reflected in the way children see their experience. And children often end up blaming themselves for the suffering of their parents. We don't want to saddle them with this additional burden of guilt.

Free yourself of the idea that divorce is someone's fault or that it means you are somehow incapable or undeserving of love and companionship. Relationships ending have a lot more to do with holdbacks, suffering and flaws in larger systems of culture and society than with individuals. There cannot be one reason or one fault that leads to a divorce. So how can it be one person's responsibility or burden of shame if that happens? Divorces often happen because entire families fail to step in and support a couple in conflict, or when economic imbalances cause rifts or when generational pain and trauma makes one partner avoid responsibilities or inflict pain. It's not one thing alone. Step back from the events of your separation

*Brown, Jeff, *Hearticulations: On Love, Friendship, and Healing*, Enrealment Press, Toronto, Canada, 2020.

and take time to examine the various things that caused the split.

When I took a wide-angle view of what happened in my marriage, I saw that it was a combination of many things. It was my childhood trauma of sexual abuse and the concomitant feelings of inadequacy, low self-worth and low self-esteem. It was my teenage depression and suicide attempt. It was my ex-husband's childhood experience of violent parenting and emotional abuse coupled with the unresolved grief from his mother's early demise. It was his sadomasochistic tendency. It was my incapacity to maintain boundaries and unfulfilled intellectual dreams. It was my ex-husband's coping mechanisms that were hurtful to me.

The failure of our marriage, if one calls it that, was also a failure on the part of both our families to protect two very young and troubled individuals from their own selves. Both of us needed help and intervention long before we married. Our families ignored that need for years, encouraged us to get married and looked the other way, despite the warnings from others around them that they were being too precipitate, hoping that the union would solve our problems. And then there is also the fact that both of us sought escape in love because it felt good, it was easier than working on ourselves. And we were too young and inexperienced to know any better. It would be too simplistic and convenient to lay the entire blame on one person

Look at your relationship with an intention to recover deleted and forgotten information that has been lost in an attempt to hold on to some shreds of self-respect, or an attempt to not take responsibility for your part in a relationship ending. Victim stories are comforting because there's always someone else responsible for your pain; but they're never complete stories. Degrees of responsibility and suffering might vary. There will always be one partner who suffers more than the other in any given circumstance.

Please find the courage to look at your present and past with the complexity that is the essence of our lives. Do this for yourself and do this so you don't pass on the feelings of failure, guilt, shame and anger to your children. And none of this is meant to invalidate or reduce your pain and suffering. But it is to also look at all the events/influences/histories that caused that. Doing this helps us step away from bitterness and blame, both of which corrode our own being more than anything else.

So, what can you reframe divorce and separation as? I have reframed mine as release, as renewal and as possibility. What parts of your marriage or relationship story have you unconsciously deleted or suppressed? And what do you discover when you attempt to retrieve that?

Trying to do divorce as gracefully as possible

When the decision is made and the arrow of separation has left the bow of your effort, there will be a clamour to claim the fallen animal; in this case your marriage. There will be a slew of angry advice and 'this is what you should do' from family members and lawyers eager to play out the drama of their own egos on the stage of your hurt. And you will feel pushed and pulled. While some relationships end in the ugly throes of vengeance because of the nature of the pain poured into it, most marriages end because of a lack of feeling. And that doesn't require an elaborate exaction of emotional dues.

But it's hard to walk away with your head held high when all the world around you, especially those supporting you in this transition, advise in a way that only piles on more hurt and trauma on both parties. It can be difficult to claim only the benefits that are needed, like financial support for children or returning wedding jewellery or dividing the wealth that had been accrued together. It is hard not to demand compensation for emotional hurt through multiple court cases and public accusations. It is hard to retain dignity about whom we disclose our affairs to and what we say about the other. It can be very tempting to vomit out all of our hurt in full public glare for all the world to see, even if it is our story alone. There is a certain relief in having our pain witnessed.

But what unpleasant repercussions will this have? In my experience, it can cause more suffering to one's self and any children involved. It can lead to more anger and bitterness than is warranted and may even impede the separation process. I was advised by folks to file cases against my ex's family. Given that I was very angry and hurt, the idea seemed tempting; to punish them for the massive lack of consideration shown to me by my ex and his family, to hurt so much that they gave me the respect I needed and deserved.

However, I had second thoughts, wondering whether I would be able to live with myself if I did file cases against my in-laws, and how my son would feel when he eventually discovered what had happened to his father and beloved grandfather. I wondered whether it was even fair to punish an entire family for the actions of one? True, they could have supported me more; yes, they could have actively reached out to my son or they could have helped me with finances. But to me it seemed like a breach of my own integrity to push false claims in court.

My lawyer warned me that this could mean the case dragging in court forever and that I may not get any financial compensation. And that did happen. Despite my discretion about the details of our marriage, there was mudslinging and name-calling and if I had gone ahead with the lawyer's suggestion, it could have only been much worse.

In most cases, given the shoddy state of family courts, cases drag on for years and even when the law is in favour of women, the people who uphold those laws do everything possible to invalidate, trivialize and ignore the concerns of women. It is hard to be dignified and subdue rage. It is hard to not want to destroy families and systems. It is hard to not want revenge. And then there are the many men who suffer at the hands of misused laws too. I know them, I know of them. None of this is black and white.

I feel the one thing that can help us as we tread this murky path is to maintain direct contact with the spouse or partner and to try and bring in empathy in the way we communicate our needs. Even that can be difficult when one partner is in denial and refuses to take responsibility for his or her actions. In that case, it becomes important that we hold counsel with those who don't spur our anger, who guide us with maturity and stability and who do not seek to right the wrongs done to them by piggybacking on our misery. Direct contact, even when it is difficult and could require one person's being more patient and calmer than the other, can possibly bring some semblance of grace into what the next best step is to ease a formal separation.

Even that may be difficult if one person is given to emotionally blackmailing and guilting the other. On the whole, it is a messy situation with no clear answers about what is best. Larger systems of families either withhold support entirely from warring couples or make the situation worse by peddling their own egos. My own lived experience has helped me appreciate patience and sustained effort to do what was best for my mental health and well-being. Some of those things were not appreciated by others, and that is okay.

Consciously refraining from passing on bitterness to children

The other thing that helped me (and continues to help both my ex and me) was to speak as little as possible about the other person, especially to outsiders. I did not want to surround myself with barbed comments or probing questions that could reach my son. I did not want to pass on my own hurt and resentment to him. I actively asked my parents to not bad mouth my ex-husband around my son. It did not go down well because they were hurting too, but my son's experience was more important to me at that time. I think the children's experience is what we forget in these situations; that the child is most vulnerable as his reality is still taking form, and he is likely to carry your experience and performance of the divorce into the way he handles relationships later. I think that the awareness of how one's handling of a crisis can shape the future will go a long way to reduce the inevitable pain that will follow. Although this is very difficult, it is crucial to try and maintain a long-term view during the crises without focusing solely on the unfolding events.

As Jeff Brown puts it beautifully:

> Those who can put a boundary around their anger at their ex, and continue to honour their children's right to love them, are making this world a healthier place.

It is important to share facts with children when they ask questions, but they need not be overwhelmed with intimate details or used as a dumping ground. And no matter what we do, unless there is real danger to the children, we have no business making decisions about who sees the children or not. They have every right to make their own decisions about how much or if at all they want to meet the other parent. Sometimes that learning will be fraught with difficulty, pain or rejection for them. But allowing them to make their own journey at least keeps them from developing prejudices and from harbouring resentments. Hurt exes often peddle personal bias as a defense against recrimination and other fallouts of a divorce. They do everything possible to not allow the meeting or the sharing of spaces between the ex and the children.

If there's one thing I regret in all the mess that followed my separation, it is not letting Imaad see his dad for two years while we were fighting in court. It is true that I had been driven to exhaustion after holding space for my ex despite my own pain, but I am truly sorry for having kept his son away from him. And I am mortified that my son suffered through all that time. I have spent the years after that trying to do everything possible to make sure that my son and his father meet, even though I've mostly been the one initiating and organising meetings at my son's behest.

Communicating clearly with your children

There are times I have wished Imaad wouldn't ask me why I separated, or why did I not love his Abba anymore. Those are perhaps the only times when my own vulnerability has threatened to break the 'cool mom' persona. But, as he grew older, I learned to answer these questions sensibly and calmly. I figured out that using more 'us' and 'we' words when talking about the reasons for our divorce helped take away any sense of blame on his dad. Early on in my separation, I had requested his dad that we use the same language and the same reasons about our decision when talking to Imu. My ex didn't always follow this protocol, but over time he saw the benefits of these rules, especially after I became dogged about it and threatened to tell the truth if he couldn't stick to our story, which was: 'Amma and Abba love you dearly. We have loved each other too, but now we no longer feel that way and it is better to stay apart than fight all the time.'

Over time, more nuances were added to this story as Imaad grew older, but the essence of it remained the same. I insisted that we say the same thing to our child so he could feel grounded and not confused. It was hard to keep track of the other things he heard about me when he visited his dad's house.

There was a time when someone told him: 'Your mother left because she is selfish, but we love her all the same.' He came back and asked me why I had done that.

My first response was rage that someone could say that. But I quickly saw that my rage wasn't going to help my son.

So, I said, yes, I was selfish, and I left because I was very unhappy. I had been unhappy for years and had tried to make things work before leaving. And I also said that everyone deserves happiness; although wanting to be happy may seem selfish to some people, happiness is important if we are to live well. I further told him that, when one person leaves, the others suffer too, and maybe that is why he heard what he did. But did he like how much calmer I was now? Did he like that I smiled more and cried less? He said yes. And that was enough for him to understand.

All of this still does not guarantee that your child will not resent you for leaving or separating. It does not guarantee that the process of realigning to a new family situation will become any easier. But paying attention to what we say, how much we say, what words we use and how we tame our own bitterness can go a long way in creating more ease for children.

Making room to grieve

Divorce and separation can be relentless. They can be like a grief that is so raw and un-homed that one doesn't know where to keep it, calm it, live it. The adults moving away from each other carry their unresolved questions, worries, fears. And for the children, this time can be so confusing. It's like all their tiny lives they have seen the sun glow yellow and the moon glow white. Their parents have shaped their sense of themselves in the world. And when that containment is broken, when family as they knew it no longer exists and home situations change drastically, all can seem lost and bleak.

I feel that we, as adults, can learn to make room for this peculiar grief for both ourselves and our children. When we allow ourselves the space to mourn through whatever is available and seems fit, we allow ourselves to essentially live out our pain, to stop carrying it like a crown of thorns. And when we do that, the relief we feel, the small steps we make towards a new reality, can help our children move too.

My teacher, Bhavana, once shared with me how she created her own ritual around her divorce. She called in her close friends to witness her transition from one suffering a separation to one honouring what was beautiful in the relationship. She wrote and shared her experience of her ex-partner and how it shaped her in beautiful ways. None of this was meant to discredit the hurt she had experienced. But it was a deep acknowledgment of all that existed in the relationship. To me, it sounded like a beautiful ritual of recovery, remembrance and resilience.

How do we move into acceptance if we don't see both the good and the bad in the past? How do we look ahead and around if one eye is covered? Grieving rituals are ways of keeping our focus on the past, the present and the future. They allow us room to say to ourselves, 'This is over. You can move on now.' Although the recovery time will vary for each person, it is important we do move on and not remain stuck in the past.

What we do, our children absorb. When we experience ourselves as not just a divorcee, but as someone capable of redefining ourselves in the world, of retelling our stories of love and loss, our children learn to do that too. So, when Imaad says that he wants to be more present for his children than his father is, I tell him that his future need not be 'what his father is not' but simply, what he, Imaad, would like to be. And to do that, I allow space for his sadness at the loss of his father in his everyday life, make room to talk about it, don't rush him to forget but encourage him to be strong and not be angry—all of this is important.

When I make room for his feelings to flow any which way, they come to rest. When he kicks his football in rage when his dad doesn't show up at important events, I don't ask him to stop. He stops on his own and asks for a hug. When he locks himself in his room after a visit to his *Dada Abba* (paternal grandfather) because he misses him so, I don't badger him to come out. He comes out on his own and asks for a cheese sandwich or a chat. When he was little, he'd grow incredibly moody around 'whole' families at events. I did not categorize that as bad behaviour. I think what helped me was to not take his reactions personally and to not see them as signs of permanent damage. I had to cultivate faith in the fact that time will change his sadness. I hope I can continue to do that.

There can be a danger of our inviting guilt when we see our children acting out of pain or anger. It is only human to hold ourselves responsible for these tantrums, but it is not helpful. It does not help to blame oneself for things that were up to many to resolve and heal. What helps is extending your lap, your arms, your silent support and the ability to make room for your child's experience of the divorce that is and will be separate from yours. There is no one victim in this story. Don't compete for who is suffering more. We all suffer when a storm breaks out. The roof leaks, the windows slam and the plants wither. The best we can do is keep each other warm, share blankets and listen to each other's stories of pain. The best we can do is make room.

Seeking and relying on community

One of the biggest things we lose when we divorce or separate is shared communities, shared friends, known homes and neighbourhoods. It is very rare to find situations where people have been able to retain common friends after separating. It's hard for anyone to walk that tight rope of staying loyal to both parties although most people don't want to take sides even when it may be needed. And then there are those that cannot take sides, like family and immediate relatives of one partner standing up for the other partner. It's just too messy. Immediate family of both people involved may be able to be objective about who is right or wrong, but it's hard to stay relevant and participate in the life of the person who leaves.

When we face this particular loss of familiar homes and people, it becomes important to create new ones, to reach out to people not directly involved in the divorce conflict and say to them, 'I need your care.' When I returned to my parents' home with little Imu in tow, eight years after my marriage, my cousins in the city stepped in to play the family. And I let them. I asked them to come play with my son or to babysit when I went to court or had to run an errand. I called my siblings to come and stay and to take care of Imaad when I just couldn't. Then there were friends in the city who sort of adopted us; who invited me to come and visit with Imaad; who made it a point to include us in picnics and festivals. Some of them are no longer part of our everyday lives, but I will remain indebted to them forever.

One can say that I am blessed and incredibly lucky to have had that much support at one of the most difficult times in my life. And it is true. I have been and continue to be blessed with support. But what is also true is that I was able to keep myself open to invitations from family and friends. And that I let go of all sense of pride in asking for support. I devoted myself fully into making time for these new families that had extended themselves to me. Sometimes it meant that I had to show up when they needed me, or that I would travel with my child to meet them. I saw the value in making that effort, both for Imaad and me, and for the friendship as well.

All of this was possible maybe because my circumstances did not require me to slog long hours in offices. There was enough cushioning from my siblings and parents to allow me time to heal. I sometimes wonder what it would have been like if Imu had to be put into day-care and I had to work full time right after the separation. Probably avenues of support would have opened up then as well. I believe that the universe works for us in mysterious ways. Doors to new opportunities keep opening and some of those doors may vanish or recede over time. But the universe stays available to us if we stay open to it. In my opinion, the aspiration for complete independence in the way we raise our children and work is both a fallacy and an injury to relationships and benefits that appear when we learn to rely on others.

Interdependence: the honouring and nurturing of the many vines that twist and twirl around us as we put down roots in new soil is literally what keeps us alive.

So that is what you do. Acknowledge that the rearing and caring of children after a divorce or separation is not on you alone. Give yourself permission to seek, ask, need. It doesn't make you weak. It only makes you human and more capable to walk this path that you are choosing or that has been chosen for you. Please remember that you won't always be this fragile or vulnerable. You won't always burst into tears at the sight of parents walking together on school open days, or families rejoicing on the beach. You won't always feel like you have been denied happiness or that it has been snatched from you. It will pass. Both for you and your children. And until such time, it is okay to want, need and ask for all the support you can get. You are not alone. A sapling needs support to grow into a strong tree, big enough to shelter birds and bear fruit. And you (man or woman), in your lonely excursion away from coupled parenting, need hands to hold on to. When you're ready, you'll watch your children revel in your shade and play beneath your branches as you remain centred and grounded.

As I look back at that time in my life when I felt like everything had collapsed and that Imaad would suffer forever because of our inability to stay together as a couple, I reflect on a few things.

One, that pain, in all its acuteness, passes. What one needs is a willingness to accept that some things are irrevocable.

Two, that two parents alone do not and cannot decide the 'outcome' of their child's life. Children seek out their own paths and nurture even when those come with pain. All we can do as parents is to keep the doors and windows of our being open to the elements that arrive as experiences, people and events.

Three, one needs an awareness of one's behaviour patterns, the thought prisons that trap one and cause one's reactions; awareness alone can bring about huge shifts in the way we repeat unhealthy patterns of behaviour before they hurt our children. Awareness alone can lead us to that wonderful albeit difficult path of healing, both for ourselves and our children.

Four, that something will probably always hurt and that is okay. What we do with all the love we want and have, despite that hurt, is what defines us.

Chapter 9

Loss and Grief

There's a beautiful book for children that explores death, *Cry, Heart, But Never Break*, by Glenn Ringtved. In the book, four very sad children sit in a dimly lit kitchen while their ailing grandmother sleeps upstairs. As they sit wondering whether their grandma will make it through the night, the Grim Reaper arrives. The finality of their grandmother's inevitable death grips the children and they implore the Reaper not to take her away. What follows in the story is a profound yet simple exploration of how children can be made to see death not as an abrupt ending, but as a passing on by allowing them room to grieve. As the Grim Reaper leaves, he tells the children to bid their grandmother's spirit goodbye and to hold on to her memory with love; he teaches them to feel sorrow without feeling despair.

As adults, somewhat hardened by life, it is hard for us to imagine what the shock of a loved one being taken away must feel like for children. It could be the loss of a beloved pet, an aging grandparent or the death of a dream or plan. For us to underestimate the effect any of these can have on a child's sense of self and the world is to set them up for bitterness, loneliness and angst. How can we hold our children better as they grieve? How do we suspend our own predicament for a while and reach down to the level of their imagination, to sit by the collective loss, together as we allow our hearts to cry, but not to break? To push children to be 'brave', to 'man up', is to take away the necessary space they need to register and mourn the loss they suffer.

Why are we here? What is the purpose of life? Why do people die? For a curious child who observes everything with an acute keenness that is often missing in adults, these questions take on a life of their own. And perhaps it is through the exploration of these questions as we observe animals, nature and space with our children, we can show (rather than tell) them the coexistence of beauty with death and decay. Animals are born and die, galaxies take shape and stars explode, storms arrive and subside; everything in nature has a beginning and an end. That is what our children need to learn. And what does that ask of us? Perhaps a widening of our hearts, a search for soothing responses and patience in the face of a child's guileless anger and despair at loss. And perhaps also a deeper understanding of why it's so hard to let anyone, especially children, mourn.

The scourge of joy

There's a very interesting section in Joan Didion's beautiful book on grieving, *The Year of Magical Thinking*. I read it repeatedly this year in the aftermath of the COVID-19 second wave to understand public attitudes towards death. This is how it goes:

> Philippe Ariès, in a series of lectures he delivered at Johns Hopkins in 1973 and later published as *Western Attitudes Towards Death: From the Middle Ages to The Present*, noted that beginning about 1930 there had been in most Western countries and particularly in the United States a revolution in accepted attitudes towards death. 'Death,' he wrote, 'so omnipresent in the past that it was familiar, would be effaced, would disappear. It would become shameful and forbidden.'
>
> The English social anthropologist Geoffrey Gorer, in his 1965 *Death, Grief and Mourning*, had described this rejection of public mourning as a result of the increasing pressure of a new 'ethical duty to enjoy oneself,' a novel 'imperative to do nothing which might hinder the enjoyment of others.'

In both England and the United States, he observed, the contemporary trend was 'to treat mourning as morbid self-indulgence, and to give social admiration to the bereaved who hide their grief so fully that no one would guess anything had happened.'*

We were neck deep in death and loss in April 2021. Images of burning pyres and piled up bodies pinged daily/hourly on our phones. Death was massive, like a wet blanket one was wrapped in; heavy and cold. And no matter how much you tried to toss, turn, run, this blanket continued to envelop you. And yet, nearly every other day someone reached out to

---

*Didion, Joan, *The Year of Magical Thinking*, London: HarperCollins, 2006.

me for 'grief counselling' for a friend or relative who had just lost a loved one. 'They are crying. They are numb. They won't eat. Please counsel them.' I would shake my head in disbelief at each phone call and try to explain to callers that grief, above anything else, takes time. It takes a long, long time to thaw into something resembling human from the animal pain it is. And that no amount of counselling or intervention could help. They had to be patient. They had to give each other time.

But they would still insist. So, I would sit through calls, talking in soft whispers, asking folks about the loved ones they had lost, recalling faces and memories, recalling gifts of presence. That often led to shattering cries and deep sobs, the kind that make you want to muffle your ears. But I would listen, I would hold the other person in my silence and let them cry. What else could I do? Surely not the 'you will get over this' and 'move on' that is the scourge of grief responses so popular today. How does one *move on* from loss, and that too so quickly? That whole period made me realize one thing down to my very bones—our inability to sit with someone's loss and grief is not a symptom of care for the other person, it is not a wish for them to recover and heal. It is a symptom of acute discomfort with any emotion that is not happiness.

Like dentists we flourish scalpels and plug root canals of misery wherever we see them-

Have you lost a doll? Let me get you another one. Why are you crying? Big children don't cry.

It was just a breakup. Get over it already!

I'm sorry your father passed away. You mustn't let it affect you. You'll be fine. You'll get over this. Just be strong.

It was a dog. You're crying like your mother died.

Why are you always so depressed? You must try harder, you know. Go out, meet friends.

Scrape, scrape, whirr—the pain keeps moving like a motor. Stop, make the pain stop.

Stop because *I* can't bear to see this.

This is how we expand our capacity for joy and only joy and like a swelling, it pushes thin its twin sister, sorrow, into the shadows. Edges it out, until there's no room for it, or us, to take shape, take form and stay whole. Like two eyes that see the world, happiness and sorrow see together and to shut one out is to make the world, our minds, our lives one dimensional. If joy is breathing in, sadness is breathing out. And yet we hold our breath and want others, especially children, to walk with clenched stomachs and purple faces until we collapse for want of release.

In your lives, for yourself and your children, at your dining tables and bedrooms, reserve a spot for sorrow. Let it enter your homes at night and in the day and let it whisper its dirges. Let it haunt your treasured spaces so it can finally leave. Denying expressions of loss in others is like being the doctor who treats a schizophrenic patient and tells him that his visions are not real. Be the doctor who believes the patient, and then helps him nurse his brain to health. Allowing for sorrow is also allowing for trust and love.

The time it takes

My first experience of death up close was when *Daadi* (paternal grandmother) passed away in 1993. I still remember the hot summer day when it happened. Daadi had made khichdi for us in the afternoon and then she took all of us up to the terrace. Terrace time was a ritual with Daadi. She would oil and braid her hair on the terrace, and we would scamper around her, playing. To this day I don't know why she chose a sweltering May afternoon to sit in the sun. Or maybe it was evening. By that night, she had suffered three massive heart attacks and was gone.

For weeks afterwards I remember wishing that she would visit me in a dream, like she visited Sadaf, my younger sister in her dreams every night. Sadaf had spent the first two years of her life attached to Daadi's hip. In my mind, she was an extension of Daadi's body, smelling of her. Glycerine and Pears soap smell mingled with the soft cotton smell of freshly starched dupattas. To say that Sadaf was devastated after Daadi's death would be an understatement. She was barely eight when it happened and for a year afterwards, the chirpy, talkative child, whom Daadi had left behind, was lost. Curled in the foetal position, wedged between sofas, or hiding under Daadi's cot in the living room; we would find her sleeping with Daadi's white dupatta wrapped tight around her hand, one thumb moving gently with her sucking lips. Grief was the empty look in her eyes all day, every day for months. Grief was the silence that trailed behind her wherever she went. For almost a year, we forgot what Saddu's laughter sounded like. Grief was a small child, drifting and uncomplaining, and falling asleep in dark corners.

I don't remember how my parents helped her cope or if we had any discussions around how to help her, if at all that was possible. What I remember is that my older sister, Saba, stepped into Daadi's shoes and became Sadaf's mother. Our own mother was overwhelmed by the demands of a growing hospital, teeming with patients on the one hand and a husband slowly recovering from a bypass surgery. What I also remember is that no one asked Sadaf why she was quiet, or why she did not eat enough, or laugh or play outside. There were no questions, no nagging, no reprimands to do this or that. No one made fun of her for going around the house with

Daadi's sweater or dupatta wrapped around her tiny frame. We just let her be. And we loved her. I don't think grief in children needs anything more than that; time is all that is needed, all the time that it takes to make sense of a loved one gone, vanished. And love; gentle, consistent and kind, the kind that doesn't ask questions or pass remarks.

Nobody teaches children how to help a sibling grieve. I think children instinctively know how to honour loss and pain. And I think the three of us knew too. We closed around Sadaf like leaves around a baby pod. We were her oyster and she rested as long as she needed to. It is the adults who get caught in the socially appropriate demonstrations of grief, who don't know what to do or say to comfort children when it comes to death. Their concern is like a sharp object that pokes. They ask children to grow up, to not fuss, to not be irritable and they worry and nag when grades fall or when school is missed. As if these things hold any space at all in the gaping universe that is a grieving child's mind. No, children cannot and should not be asked to be okay when they lose a family member, a pet, a friend or a dear relative. They can't be okay until they naturally are. All we can do is allow them to take the time that it takes. We can protect them from nagging school authorities and caustic relatives. We can let unimportant things slide. We can offer endless hugs and also contain them when they go rejected. Grief in children is also anger and confusion. And that needs room too. It cannot be explained or shouted away. It can only be held.

The form it takes

When Imaad was little, I often wondered how I would explain things like death to him. I need not have worried. A child who chooses to surround himself with life will inevitably chance upon death, even if it is too close for comfort. In the winter of 2019, Imaad began 'rescuing' older dogs, puppies, birds, cats, any animal he felt needed help in our area. I tried to dissuade him knowing that I did not have the space, patience and funds to take care of animals. But a twelve-year-old, who sees himself as a rebel and a rescuer, can be intractable.

By January of 2020, three dogs, including a bow-legged ancient granny bitch, were permanent residents of our compound. In February of the same year, Imaad found Chocolate on one of his daily dog-feeding rambles in the neighbourhood. A tiny, brown puppy with the warmest brown eyes I have ever seen, which had been stuck in coal tar and badly injured. He was one of several pups fending for himself by a roadside restaurant and was yelping in agony when Imaad brought him home.

One look at the tiny creature, and I knew we were in deep trouble. Despite visits to the vet and efforts to feed and clean him up, the pup did not survive. Imaad was inconsolable. He insisted on digging Chocolate's grave himself and I let him. For days, he would mourn beside the small grave and weep. He would lock himself in his room, refuse food and yell at me when I tried to comfort him. After a week of screaming, crying, nightmares and skipping school, I refused to leave until he told me what else was bothering him besides the fact that the pup had not survived. To my shock, Imu told me that he felt that Chocolate had died because of him—because he could not help him and because caring for the sick pup had tired him so much that, at one point, he had wished that the poor thing would die.

I don't know which emotion I felt more strongly, tenderness at his young heart that had hoped that he could save the puppy, or anger at myself for exposing Imaad to a situation that he was not prepared to handle. I comforted him as best I could and asked Imu what might make him feel better.

'I want Chocolate to know I did not want him to die, Amma. I didn't want him to die.'

I asked him to write a letter to Chocolate, saying that those who leave us can hear our thoughts and read our letters. I wanted whatever he was feeling to find an outlet, a release in any form.

The next day, Imu showed me a note he had written about Chocolate on his iPad and I saved it. This is what it said:

THE STORY OF CHOCOLATE

You were the spark of my life. You taught me that however long or short our life is, it is important to live life to its fullest. You were and are loved; you will always be remembered. We miss you, Chocolate.

Chocolate was my boy; the one being I fell in love with the moment I saw his face and no matter how dirty or crippled he was, I loved him so much. I couldn't stop blaming myself for letting him die. Although Amma told me it wasn't my fault, even today I feel responsible for his death because I forgot to give him his medication on the night before his death. On the day he turned two months old, he died.

He was rescued from the front of a hotel where a car had run over him, breaking his ribs and crippling his left hind leg. My kind friends, who worked in that hotel, took care of him, knowing that I would come by to feed the stray animals in the area. When they saw me, they asked whether I could help him. I fell in love with the little pup the moment I laid eyes on him. I did not hesitate and took him home at once.

My best friend Fateh, my mother and I took turns to care for him for the ten days he was with us. Two nights before the incident, my mother left for Delhi for a meeting she had to attend.

The thing I feel most guilty about is that, although a part of me was grieving, another part of me was glad he had died. Later, I was mortified at having even thought such a thing. I talked to Amma about it and she explained that I was just in shock.

Now I feel that he is happier up there in dog heaven knowing that he was loved until the end.

And it makes me rest easier knowing my best friend is happy now and can run free without any limits.

—Imaad Zaidi

To this day, I don't know what prompted me to ask Imaad to write. I just knew that he needed to give some form of expression to his bottled-up grief because it couldn't be conveyed through conversation or released with his tears. It is a human need, especially in children to be able to touch, see and make sense of loss. Confusion, rage, despair and helplessness at the remorselessness of life and death—all of these gigantic happenings are made understandable when they take the form of a drawing, a prayer, a poem, a card, a mud figurine or a clay sculpture. Anything that somehow houses the restlessness within tiny chests, gives it meaning and can be reached is perhaps reassuring to children. Like mementos: photographs and gifts from loved ones long gone are precious for adults. In neat nests of love, they contain the vast waves of our emotions when a loved one leaves. In shaping, writing, making and drawing them, little ones can come home to the lost friend, pet or family member. Or so I feel.

Children cannot be burdened with complicated answers about life and death, and I don't feel it is sensible to placate them with myths and tall tales that they will question later. A lot of children can feel betrayed or cheated when they are told to 'Ask God to return xyz to you' or 'If you are a good boy/girl, God will give xyz back'. And worst of all is telling children something or someone was taken away because they were 'bad'. I feel it is cruel to burden a tiny heart with such guilt. It speaks volumes about a culture which conflates shame with loss of life, limb, love, marriage or job. It is unkind to inflict our own ideas of divine retribution on innocent minds. The best we can do is give children the tools to express their feelings, however they can or want to do. Our job is to teach them how to let go, experience and make room for sadness so that they can breathe easier.

Imaad still misses Chocolate and often places pieces of Parle-G biscuits on his grave. I don't tell him that the birds will eat them or that dead puppies do not eat. After the day he wrote the note, he was calmer and less angry. It took the time it took, but something in him eased through his writing that eulogy.

When needed, become a wall

One can wax eloquent about how to support children when they are grieving or how to make sense of loss, but sometimes, life puts one in situations when you realize that you know you can do nothing except try and protect yourself

or your children as best as you can. In April 2018, a very
close family friend A, lost her husband. A was in shock and
so were her three children. All around her, folks were telling
her to 'stay strong' for her children and that she had to be
'their mother and father now.' I don't know what to make of
such inane platitudes. Perhaps people don't understand the
acid corrosiveness of such inane statements because they
have not known loss themselves. Or perhaps it is a culturally
appropriate thing to say to a young widow and no one has
really thought about how stupid it sounds. Try as she might,
she can never be both mother and father for her children, and
in order to be a good enough mother for them, she would
need to live out her own grief too.

As her friends, we were helpless, and we did not know
how to be of any use to her. I remember the day we brought
her husband's body home and there was loud lamenting
everywhere. This tiny, frail woman, who had seen absolute
hell in the past month turned to us and said, 'I want you to
protect my children. Be around them, stick by them. Let no
one tell them to grow up or be brave or drown them in their
own tears. Guard them and give them what they need.'

I was amazed at her clarity of thought and to this day I
admire the way she held herself as proof against those who
were strangers to her children. She would ask her children who
they needed around them and it would usually be one of her
friends. Only those select few were let inside their rooms. The
children were not forced to sit for the ceremonies or coerced
to see visiting relatives. They were given whatever they asked
for in terms of food or the company they wanted.

To this day, I don't know whether it was the right thing
to do to force the children to see their father's dead body
before it was taken to the cremation ground and see the
burning pyre. It was certainly not their mother's idea, but

in Indian households, where rituals are decreed and decided by elders, there is very little a young widow can stand up to. I remember just holding on to A's words and staying with her children. Three close friends held each of the children and walked them through a horde of lamenting relatives. We sat with them, at a safe distance from the burning pyre and no one compelled them to watch. They held on to us, sobbing and numb. And we held them. There's little else one can do at a time like this. What story, what word, what ritual can comfort a child faced by the grisliness of seeing a beloved body burn?

'Why are they burning Daddy, Reema aunty?' one of A's girls asked me as she watched the flames. She had always been quiet and serious and I was not surprised by her question.

'So that he can turn into smoke and mingle with the air, sweetheart. That way he will become a part of the sky and remain around you always,' I replied, pointing to the dark cloud of smoke rising from the pyre. I have no clue why I said that or what it meant or if it helped her in any way. All I know is that children may not always understand rituals or religion. But they understand elements and how they move and touch us. They understand animals and nature and the moon and the sun as easily as they recognize warmth and kindness. I don't know what other language to use when children ask me questions to which I have no answers. So, I use the language of the body and how it smells, tastes, feels, sees. The language that is comprehensible to children from the moment they are born. In that knowingness, some of their confusion is laid to rest, some of their questions, answered. I have no other way of saying how I know this except for the memory of how the child folded herself softly into my belly after I answered her question. Her face on the mound of my stomach, hands holding on to my sides, my body knew that she understood; what or how I cannot say.

In the days and weeks that followed that death, we almost lived in A's house. Our children rested and played with hers. We ate together and often curled up in bed and watched TV together. Sometimes A would lead me by the hand to a separate room, shut the door behind her, put her face in my lap and howl. I would let her. No word, no thought, no action was going to make it okay for her or her children. All we could do was offer the comfort of our bodies, our shoulders, our arms. We would order food and eat together. We ordered delicious street food, pizzas and desserts and just ate. It didn't matter that the family disapproved or that folks thought it was unseemly to gobble up golgappas so soon after a death in the family. We did what was needed, what the body needed. It didn't matter what culture or society deemed appropriate. Nothing you did or said would change events or repair the irreparable loss. Comfort is all one can offer and hope for. I don't see who gets to decide what is okay or not except the bereaved and grieving. Ask and offer has been my way of supporting whoever has needed comfort around me. I think it works most of the time.

Later, when A moved to another city and we would catch up, I would ask her how her children were coping. Her youngest talked about his father all the time while the older children pretended like he never existed. Perhaps their ages also explained the way they chose to actively remember or 'forget' their father. I remember something A said to me in one of those conversations. She said, 'I can only try, Reema. I can tell them I am here and maybe I can take them to therapy later, but they will take the time they take and when they do confront, or process their grief, how they do it will also be up to them. I can't do much except keep them safe, fed and clothed.' I don't think anything can explain the helplessness or wisdom of a parent when talking about the limitations of their presence more clearly than this.

Perhaps one of the things adults need to remember when grappling with how to help their children with loss is that we can only do so much despite our best intentions. When I think about the loss Imaad has felt through separation from an extended family through my divorce, it makes sense to me too. There is no comparison here between our loss and A's bereavement, but there is a sameness in the limitation. She could only do so much with the thousand things that she had to take care of in the wake of her husband's death. And I could only do so much after my divorce. It was not up to me to make sure that Imu's family from his dad's side kept in touch or visited. I could keep my doors open and invite them in at the most. The rest was up to them. And no one came or called except for the one time that I pleaded because Imu missed his grandfather so much. I would take him with me to visit, arrange drop offs and pickups to aunts' and uncles' places, I would ask him to call everyone regularly but when faced with nothing but silence, I couldn't do much other than hold my child through his peculiar loss.

Over the years, Imu has continued to ask me why no one, except his dad visits; why no one attends his birthday parties despite invitations; and why no one calls or sends gifts except when he visits on occasion. I have been very tempted to give vent to my own feelings of abandonment by the family and tell him that maybe no one cares. But what would that make me? Instead, I tell him that maybe they don't want to face my parents after everything that had happened; or maybe they are busy; or that his grandfather is too old to travel; and that his uncle is too busy with his own toddler and work. I don't think he buys any of that. Especially because he sees my siblings and their spouses go out of their way to make him feel loved and remembered. They always call on his birthday and take him out when they visit. My close friends, whom I don't even meet very often, call regularly and keep in touch with him knowing how much he needs the village to make him feel at home. My cousins WhatsApp him and they share memes on Instagram. He can see the huge difference between the way the two limbs of his family contribute or withhold from his experience of family, and that crushes him.

There's nothing for me to do but hold him when he cries and hope that, in time, he will understand the complexity of this particular kind of loss and grief. No explanation can simplify the tangled web of behaviours and relationships that happen post-divorce in families. He will suffer through it and I will have to watch. I can only hope that age and maturity will ease some of his pain. I can try and not add to it by inflicting my own bitterness on his suffering. Sometimes, when anger seeps into me, I show my frustration and then my heart collapses when I see him shrink. None of this is his fault just as no bereavement that happens to children is their fault. It is not fair on our part to feed them the contorted, thorny scripts of how we have been wronged. It is about our children and as parents and carers we would benefit from learning to separate our pain from theirs.

Perhaps with this demarcation, there will be room for the young ones to curl up and cry until love and life nudges them to get up and run, play and laugh again. We can only trust and hope in that with humility. Knowing that there is not much we can do, we can still try and do that much more to let them know that they are not alone. And perhaps that is enough.

Chapter 10

Emotions and Mental Health

Sometimes I feel children are like rivers, controlled from the time they emerge as hesitant trickles. At every bend and curve, their flow is manoeuvred, as if there are various dams installed in their path. Sometimes they are reduced to a slow trickle, at other times forced to gush at ferocious speeds and often blocked completely. Parents are the sluice gates to these rivers, controlling when these rivers flow and how much water they carry, directing them towards outcomes—outcomes that have been set by larger systems that dictate what is and what isn't appropriate. Their natural paths diverted, their flow controlled, I wonder if these rivers forget their joyful abandon or if these gates and bunds cause the angry floods we often see.

It is so easy to think in metaphors because they're neat and lend a seamless image to an idea or thought. But when you think of children themselves, contained in beautiful, compact bodies, it is hard to imagine the depths and range of emotions they feel. It's difficult to understand what goes on inside their little minds, how they see the world and how it affects them. But I imagine that they don't really like being told how to feel or think, just as they would feel restricted in tight clothing that hampers free movement. But this world is in the form of tight-clothing, replete with rules for everything: how to sit with backs straight, how to walk in a straight line, how to speak in class without answering back or shouting, expressions categorized as good, bad or naughty. We, as parents, do most of this categorizing because appearances matter so much to us that we blindly abide by all the social and cultural norms that decide what is and isn't acceptable. But like anything else in nature, when you put too much pressure on something that naturally flows and bounces, it can rebound quite violently.

In this section, I will share some insights that have helped me respond to my son's emotional states better. Awareness of what's inside me makes any situation better or worse and what I can do better that will guide him (as opposed to controlling him) has made me feel more at ease as a parent and him, freer and more comfortable with me. This isn't about discipline or 'ten ways you can make your child behave better', or even about why children do what they do (that is a separate book in itself, I think), but more about some things we *can* do and keep in mind that will make our children feel seen and heard; something that is a primal need in us as humans. And since this is more about my experience with my son, this is definitely not a one-size-fits-all solution, but I'm hoping there's something here that each of you can take away.

Your child's behaviour is not always about you

I remember this episode of high emotional drama with Imaad when he was seven. My older sister, Saba's family was visiting and her husband's nephew, whom Imaad was, and is, very fond of, was also there. The boys were all playing, and it ended up in a bit of rough play. I heard my brother-in-law bawling out that Imaad had hurt his nephew. He was brought to me like a criminal brought in for questioning; at that moment, I felt like we had been put in the glare of a huge spotlight as everyone watched.

I was newly separated at the time and very diffident about my abilities as a single parent. Every tantrum that Imaad threw, every time he screamed or refused to eat felt to me like it was being viewed as a personal failure on my part. In those moments, all these self-accusations screamed in my head: you're a terrible mother and you've made a right royal mess of teaching him to even behave himself. How shameful! What will people think?

I felt so ashamed that I failed to notice how terrified Imaad looked. I failed to pay attention to what he was saying or to take him aside and ask him what had happened. In the face of so much condemnation and the wailing kid before me, I felt paralysed. All my senses turned inwards, the voices in my head growing louder and louder and I slapped him. I hit my child so hard that my hand stung.

I wish that episode had never happened, and it took me a long, long time to forgive myself. My son forgave me as soon as I apologized. My tears were enough to melt his little heart. That is how deeply children love; in an instant they can forgive the hurt we cause them while we remind them over and over again of the mistakes they make. It's hard to share this incident here but I think sharing is an acknowledgment of learning, or an effort to learn more. Later, when I thought about what happened—I remember the way I froze and then reacted impulsively, without calmly taking stock of the situation—I was grateful that that moment appeared to reveal my biggest fear, my deepest vulnerability: *that I was a bad parent, that I would never be good enough for my son.* That revelation helped me see how my fear interfered with my responses to outbursts or tantrums. In those tricky moments, my internalized shame at what I perceived to be failure is what governed my response to a volatile situation with my son. And that was unhealthy, to say the least, but it could also be dangerous.

When we conflate what our child does or says with how we feel at that moment in time, we're not responding to the child's needs anymore. We're responding to what we're feeling. Most statements like, 'How dare you? You wouldn't do this if you loved me! I have taught you better!' emerge from our own lack or how we see our success as parents in any given situation. The focus shifts to the 'I' hurting inside and not to the situation at hand. There's a reason why this happens so much. In a culture where your success or failure as a parent is measured by how well behaved your child is, we internalize the checklists that measure our children. And when our children 'fail' to tick the boxes, we feel that we have failed as parents. It's no wonder that tantrums in supermarkets or squabbles at children's parties make us, the parents, feel like we've failed the math test and are being publicly admonished at the school assembly. Our world revolves around society's approval and it is very hard work to separate our responses from whether that approval has been met or denied.

It has taken me a lot of practice to retrain my brain and learn to focus on my child or whatever has happened with him and not react to the voices in my head. Here are some of the things that have helped me:

- **Identifying what triggers me to feel provoked/ shamed/challenged has helped me to separate my**

own reactions from what my child needs in a given moment. For example, I realized that my mother's carping about things that Imaad had done or said, while I was away from home, almost always made me angry and I would lash out at Imu. The fact that my mother complained as soon as I returned didn't help either. I would feel this rush of anxiety and shame and I would explode. So, I set boundaries with my mother so that she waited until I had met Imu and had spent some time with him after returning home before telling me if he had done something 'naughty'. That helped me separate the behaviour from the child and I was able to respond gently and with love. This way, Imaad didn't feel attacked or humiliated. This is just one example to help you identify that there can be things that happen repeatedly in a certain context that trigger something in us and we just react without considering why the child may be doing what he or she is doing.

- **Taking a moment to pause and breathe before responding in a high stress moment**. When there's shouting and screaming or someone has been hurt and you're needed to mediate, taking a short moment to breathe deeply and connect with your body can help calm nerves and assess any situation. It took me a while to learn this. Now we take time out regularly when things get heated and come back to discuss an issue that may be contentious. It really helps, especially now that Imaad is older. This can often look like your stepping aside for a moment or saying something like, 'Let us pause for a minute and come back to this. We're both too upset right now. We don't want to hurt each other.' Most of the time we are able to resolve things amicably.

With younger children, this can mean that you might have to place one hand on your chest and one on theirs and ask them to breathe deeply as you do the same. Saying things like, 'how about we calm down a little and then we can talk' often helps. With even younger children like toddlers, saying things like, 'it's all right', in soothing tones and offering a hug, some water or simply saying that you know they're upset and it's okay, allows children time to process what they're feeling while also feeling understood. It also gives the parent time to relax and see what the best way to respond is.

- **I have learned that when my child flounces out and slams the door behind him, it is best if I don't follow him immediately**. There was a time when I would do that, but it only made the situation worse. Imaad would stalk off in frustration, leaving in mid-discussion, when he felt I didn't understand or when I repeatedly refused him something. He still does this at times. Every time I immediately followed him to complete the conversation, things only became worse because, I realized, I wasn't following him to resolve the issue, but because I felt insulted that he had walked out on me. In a way, I made the situation about me, not about supporting him in a difficult moment. When I gave him time to cool off, I increased the chances that he would come out on his own so that we could talk things over in a calmer frame of mind. If he didn't, I would go to his room a little later, knock and ask if we could talk and enter the room if he said yes. If he refused, I left saying that he could come talk to me whenever he was ready and follow through by not nagging and nudging repeatedly.

I realize that this is very hard to do, especially when there's a pressing concern and you're worried, but it really helps especially when the children grow older. They feel respected and in control, which is what we often forget to make them feel. With teenagers, this is crucial because their sense of self is consolidating, and they learn to navigate inner and outer conflicts well if we give them space and also allow ourselves a break to think things through.

- **Reminding myself that my child's emotions and how they manifest are not always about me or a reflection of how good, or bad, a parent I am**. I think this has been the hardest thing for me to realize, articulate and remember, even inside my head. When Imaad was very young, I would go into a tizzy of 'what am I doing wrong?' every time he bawled nonstop or threw a tantrum without being able to tell me what he needed exactly (something that most young children struggle with). And this did not help at all with my low self-esteem. It made me feel bad about myself and prevented me from focusing on Imaad. I taught myself to reframe the thought in my head to 'what can I do to help him?' and that itself would open up options and I would no longer feel stuck. It wasn't easy and took a lot of practice, but with time it helped me move quickly in a messy situation. Asking questions like: tell me what you feel; where it hurts; and what I can do for you; can help if a small child is

hurt, angry, crying or very emotional and you don't
know what has happened. It also teaches children
to use language to express themselves and they feel
less helpless. Children themselves often don't know
what's bothering them and helping them find words
for feelings can make them feel empowered. This
process, when done repeatedly over time, can also
make you feel stronger as a parent because you start
witnessing a change. You begin to refocus from your
feelings in a situation to what your child needs. That,
in itself, is very liberating for parents whose default is
to blame themselves every time there is a meltdown.

- **Reminding myself that there is context to what
children are going through and some things are
merely a phase**. There have been three distinct
phases in Imaad's life so far, during which I have
really struggled with how he expresses himself
emotionally—one when he was five, the second, from
between the ages of eight and ten and the third, the
current phase, when he is fourteen. When I look back
at the phases in the past, I can clearly see that Imaad's
behaviour at the time (a lot of shouting, hitting other
children and uncontrollable bursts of rage) was clearly
a reflection of what was happening around him. In
the first phase, we had just left his paternal home and
he was struggling with the loss of his grandfather's
loving presence. He stopped eating and would cry
in his sleep apart from being very angry and lashing
out at me a lot. His entire world, as he knew it, had
collapsed. Every time he reacted or expressed himself
in the presence of a new person, I would hear things
like 'Your child is so *badtameez* (badly behaved)' or

'He is so fussy! Why don't you discipline him?' or the worst possible one '*hamare zamaane mein to bachche chun bhi nahi karte the* (kids wouldn't even squeak in our time)'. Needless to say, these comments crushed my self-esteem as a parent, hurting all the more because they often came from relatives. But what the child was feeling and expressing were his sadness and grief at the changes in his life, changes that he'd take years to fathom; they were not about my parenting abilities at all. They were all about our circumstances.

In the second phase, during which Imaad went through spells of deep gloom and frequent bouts of anger, he was constantly being bullied at school. His teachers were not supportive, and I had no way of changing schools at the time. Again, anyone who saw him during one of his 'moods' (as everyone took to calling them), would comment on how badly behaved he was. It broke my heart. How quick we are to label children, not realizing that children are like mirrors. Sometimes they mirror what they see around them, and at other times they reflect the scars on their souls. It took so much support from my siblings and my therapist at that time for me to separate his emotions from what I felt was a lack in me. I think that's a mistake a lot of parents make, and this prevents us from being present for our children in the way they need us.

I remember going to this workshop on parenting in 2018 where the trainer, whose name I cannot remember no matter how hard I try, said this beautiful thing: 'We have to learn to be vessels for our children's emotions.' Sometimes they'll need a vessel as big as a boat and at other times, even a small cup will do. That is something that has stayed with me ever since. Our job is to be able to somehow contain the turbulence our children experience without letting it unmoor us. In that sense we have to learn to be our own anchors; find friends and support systems who can bolster our belief in ourselves, who can hold us when we fumble and guide us when we are lost. If we keep seeing our child's behaviour as a measure of our worth, we will keep doing them and ourselves a great disservice.

Don't let your worry be a dark cloud

Children surprise me with their wisdom in so many ways and yet they don't. Unsullied by the idioms in which the world clothes and constricts us, they are able to see the soul of people and their problems; their keen eyes translate feelings into words so simply and quickly. These days I am very worried about Imaad's grades and school attendance. He has always struggled with school, and I have struggled with allowing us both alternative means of learning. The fear of doing yet another thing that marks me as an outsider in mainstream society is too much for me to choose differently. And sometimes my fear comes out as nagging and scolding Imaad about homework and tests.

In his third and most difficult phase (yet), when he is, even as I write, trying to make sense of his relationship with his father as a teenage boy, my scolding about school and grades makes him feel more isolated and misunderstood. Often our arguments end with a loud, 'You don't understand, Amma!!' And lately I realize that I really don't understand what it is like to be him. I have always had siblings around me, growing up. I had the safety and comfort of my brother and two sisters—people who understood me better than anyone ever did. His experience of being in two places at once, defined more by the lack and the withholding of a father than by my presence, is his alone. I cannot understand it. What are grades and school for a child who feels abandoned? And yet my worry pinches at me and I explode sometimes.

After one such explosion recently, I was trying to explain to Imaad why I nag him or why I am worried about school. He nodded his head quietly and said to me, 'Amma, I understand that you are worried. But can you try and worry in a way that doesn't hurt me?' It took me a whole moment to understand what he meant. When I nag and scold, I sometimes slip into making assumptions about what's in his head or what he has or has not done. I hate to admit that I have often called him 'lazy' and 'disorganized' while scolding him. To any child that kind of name-calling will be hurtful. I remember how it used to hurt me.

We let our worries twist our tongues and slip out as barbs that maim little hearts. We let our worries become so big and dark that we forget that time passes and bad phases end. We imagine that these dark clouds stretch all the way to eternity and the struggles we see in our children, as manifested in their emotions and behaviour, will stay forever. We imagine that the way things are now will decide their future. And we measure that future with our own past. Things that were important when we were children, good grades and clearing entrance tests, these are the yardsticks by which we measured our futures. And we couldn't have been more wrong. In a world that is changing at a speed faster than anything we have ever experienced, the archaic markers of the old territories cannot define a new territory that shapeshifts constantly; this world has changed even more radically post-pandemic. There are no maps to this age except those of curiosity and innovation, both of which children have in abundance if we unleash them. I think what we need as an antidote to our worry is courage. Courage alone can help us withstand the storms in our children's lives without floundering and foundering.

What we need is not new rules and new maps, but freedom from the fears that our children will not succeed if they don't excel in studies, if they are not class toppers and if they don't do twenty other extra-curricular activities in a week. What we need is to see this story of success and failure society has sold us for the mirage it is. How long will we keep worrying about tangible things, like money, while letting go of abstract qualities like joy and freedom? When I see Imaad struggle, be angry, mope, rebel, I tell myself: 'Mad heart, be brave!'* And that lifts away my worry like a kite. The wind then decides what it does with this kite—and lets it soar, dip or disappear. Whatever this kite does, it cannot cloud my child's sky and it most certainly cannot hurt him.

Why so serious?

I have always been an advocate of taking children seriously; seriously enough to be mindful of what they say and do and of what we say and do around them. The way we are with children is a reflection of the way we were brought up, the way we were imprinted with relationships and our childhood

---

*Shahid Ali, Agha, *Mad Heart Be Brave: Essays on the poetry of Agha Shahid Ali* edited by Kazim Ali. Michigan: University of Michigan Press, 2017.

fears, insecurities, wishes, hopes and dreams. Many of our current hopes and dreams for our children belong in the past and may not fit this present time we have with our children; in light of that, I would recommend to parent our children by looking ahead and not looking back at our pasts. That means, we may have to pay serious attention to our inner landscapes, our childhoods and how much of those we project on to our children. However, there is a problem with being too serious.

A lot of new-age parents spend so much time agonizing over everything their children say or do with the lens of 'Are they okay? Is this a symptom of some serious underlying problem with my child? What do I do now? Will this last forever?' These questions are important but if this is how your mind works most of the time around your children, I think you may be taking yourself too seriously.

What do I mean by this? There's so much jargon around parenting now where every little thing is evaluated and cross-evaluated that sometimes we lose our sense of humour in the way we look at our children or even in the way we look at parenting itself. We begin to take ourselves so seriously almost as if we are the only influence our kids will ever have and we alone get to decide the outcomes in their lives and how they 'turn out'. I don't think that's true. We are important as parents, and we will often be the most impactful in our children's lives be it in terms of the love and support they receive or the pain they undergo. But there are things that our children will do and say, ways in which they will behave, that have very little to do with us and everything to do with the developmental phase the child is in, the larger trends in society and the culture or even world events.

Take teenage, for example. On the surface, most parents joke about how difficult adolescence and teenage is; but, if you were to watch them covertly, you will find that most of them are mentally wringing their hands and suffering pangs of low self-esteem like never before. And they're having awful thoughts about their children's future. 'Just look at their manners; they'll never be able to have good relationships. They never want to talk to us or spend time with us; they don't love us; children these days don't care; there's no hope for us in our old age, etc., etc.'

It's like there's a doomsday scenario in their heads which grows increasingly morbid. What we forget is to take the phases in our children's lives lightly or to try and remember how we were as teenagers and chuckle. None of the shenanigans we did as young adults lasted long and most of us managed to grow up and become boring adults. Not everything your teenager does is a sign of his or her turning into a criminal!

Recently my son has been asking my dad and me whether he can cycle to school or buy a Scooty. Any mention of this sends my dad into a monologue of, 'Oh no, he's going to get hurt; he'll lose interest in his studies and start roaming everywhere with his friends; he'll become wild,' and so on and so forth. It takes me to remind him that he was riding a Yezdi motorbike cross-country in his late teens; my brother used to cycle to school and half the girls in my school rode a Scooty to school and to tuition classes at age fourteen or fifteen. Of course, times are different now and there's a lot more traffic and a general lack of safety, but I really don't feel the world has ever been safe for children. There were a lot fewer options earlier unlike today with the school buses and school vans; in those days, children would walk or cycle to school all the time. So, a desire to have a bicycle doesn't necessarily mean '*ladka haath se nikal gaya* (this kid is spoilt)'. That kind of outlook can dampen the environment at home and create anxiety and stress for children and their parents. Looking at things in perspective, remembering our own desires or habits when we were younger and laughing at those memories can help lighten the marathon that parenting is. Just as all toddlers who break things don't necessarily grow up to be destructive, or all children who play video games don't necessarily become international assassins later in life, children dreaming of owning a bike or a scooter are not necessarily plotting a rebellion. Most of them are going through perfectly natural phases in growing up and that shouldn't make us worry needlessly.

There's a quote from Erma Bombeck, my favourite writer on all things parenting that says,

> Our teenagers withdrew to their bedrooms on their thirteenth birthday and didn't show themselves to us again until it was time to get married.*

I think that's the kind of humour we often need to help us make sense of our children's lives and phases. Erma shows this incredible wit when she writes about children that tells us she is watching her kids closely but is not wholly consumed by what she sees. To paraphrase what she has said about how children change from when they are younger to when they become teenagers,

> Younger children are a lot like dogs. They are all over you, they want endless pats and cuddles and are always asking for treats, they want you to walk them all the time and have

---

*Bombeck, Erma, Bil Keane, *Just Wait Till You Have Children of Your Own*, Fawcett Crest, 2011.

tantrums if you leave. But when they become teenagers, they mysteriously turn into cats. They'll come to you only when they want to and not when you call them. Most of the time they'll be sleeping or hiding in dark rooms and they'll come out to eat the food you leave on trays outside their dens. We have to get used to this strange metamorphosis knowing that this isn't our doing and both the cat and the dog are actually the same child, albeit changed drastically. The best we can do is change from dog to cat parent without letting it crush us.

I think that's the most hilariously accurate description of the changes in children from childhood to adolescence/teenage emotionally and physically I've ever read. I think we'd be wise to follow suit and not be too sombre about the changes and the behaviour in our children, unless of course something drastic happens.

Try not to label your kids

I had this way of zoning out in the middle of conversations when I was younger. My siblings would be talking about an event at school or gossiping about relatives and I would say something out of context like, 'It's raining outside.' Then there were these games I had made up for myself where I would talk to keys and pretend they were two women talking to each other. The keys were called Mrs Sharma and Mrs Verma; they were neighbours and spent a lot of time drinking tea. I think I lived a lot in my imagination and the way I expressed things was different from the way my siblings or other children of my age expressed themselves. My parents often called me 'strange' or 'weird', as did my siblings. While I don't blame them (I confess I was very strange in many ways and still am), I do feel that hearing myself described by these adjectives when I was growing up made me feel like I was somehow not okay; that I was different and in a bad way. I remember feeling like that for a long time until I found friends who were a lot like me, but that was only after I was well into my thirties. I don't think anyone around me meant these comments negatively, but repeatedly hearing certain words began to hurt a lot.

What children express are just signs of how they experience their inner and outer reality and not necessarily something that can be called 'a personality trait'. I feel that this kind of repeated labelling on our part, especially of emotional reactions, can cause children to feel that there's something intrinsically wrong with them; it prevents us from considering their responses as spontaneous reactions and not a permanent peculiarity in them. It's a very tricky zone because all of us use descriptive words when we talk about children; and I have been guilty of labelling my son as 'angry' and 'loud' myself. But I do try to pay attention. In fact, it has taken Imaad's telling me how this makes him feel unheard and blamed, for me to try and be more careful with my choice of words when I refer to anything he does and says.

Some folks may think that this is extreme and that we can't be walking on eggshells around our children or that we'll make them 'too sensitive' if we always pussyfoot around them. But I think the biggest positive about avoiding labelling behaviour is that it allows us to stay in the moment and respond to our children, keeping in mind what's going on in their minds at particular points in time. It also helps us to not assume that they 'always' do this or that or to assume that they mean something when they may be thinking or feeling something entirely different.

Last night, I noticed Imaad walking around with a very glum face after my cousin and aunt, who had been visiting, left. He is usually very sensitive around people leaving and it takes him days, and sometimes weeks, to feel like himself again, especially if it's someone he adores—like my sister and her children. So Imaad came into my room and told me that he was feeling sad, and wished he didn't have to go to school the next day and asked if he could stay home. The first thought in my head was, 'Oh, no! He's going to miss school again, just as he did when my sister left, and he's going to be very upset and mopey. Why is he so sensitive? This is so hard to handle.'

I didn't say this aloud and had the sense to ask him what was making him sad. To which he replied that it had been six months since the day he first spoke to his crush and now she wasn't speaking to him, and he hated going to school and seeing her every day. He missed talking to her. Seeing patterns everywhere and assuming that a behaviour means the exact same thing every time can often prevent us from really listening to what a child needs in a difficult emotional state. I'm glad I didn't blurt out my thoughts at that moment and instead listened patiently and held Imu until he was okay.

The sea washes up flotsam and jetsam on to the beach and none of those things define the sea. It remains vast, beautiful and mysterious. Our children's moods do not define who they are or who they will be. Moods are just what the sea washed ashore. Collect them like treasures or listen to them like we do with seashells. It is likely you will hear a different song each time.

When you find yourself floundering, admit it and seek help

The biggest mistake parents make is to assume that they alone are responsible for the well-being of their children, that they know best how to heal and protect them. That is the biggest fallout of believing blindly in independence as individuals and family units. People need people, we need others to help and guide us, there are others who are trained in understanding the minds of children and how to help them much, much better than us. What we need to believe in is the power of interdependence; the ability to grow roots, tendrils and branches through soil and become creepers that reach upwards and skywards by holding on to one another. The word dependence has become a slur these days, almost as if we were brought into this world to be dropped off on a remote island and fend for ourselves alone. We weren't. To weigh down others so much that they get burdened is not okay, but to hold a hand when you're on a slippery slope with your child is what you need. Don't deny yourself that. You'll save yourself and your child a few fractures and a lot of pain.

If you see certain disturbing behaviours in your children for an extended period of time, behaviours like aggression and violent anger, long bouts of sadness and weeping, or nocturnal experiences like bed wetting and nightmares, not wanting to leave their room, repeatedly refusing to go to school or play and difficulty in following instructions or completing tasks on their own, seeking professional help is a good idea. Please remember that one-off incidents don't mean that there is something wrong with your child. In any case there's nothing wrong with your child. They're probably experiencing something they don't have the words to express, and confusion or tiredness can often be manifested as anger or frustration.

Bullying in schools and at home by older siblings or cousins, abuse at home or elsewhere, change of homes, change in family structure and routine, loud noises, accidents, loss of a pet or loved one, a friend moving away, news of political strife or shootings, witnessing a traumatic episode like a funeral or seeing something violent or frightening; there are so many events that are commonplace for adults but are life altering for children. Their experience of the world changes drastically and they may not be able to make sense of such events and may lead to deep insecurity and loneliness. They cannot adapt as easily as you can. Sometimes, I wonder whether even we, adults, adapt easily or only pretend to do so, suppressing all our inner turmoil and whistling on low octaves like pressure cookers waiting to erupt? Don't ignore repeated signs in your children that there is something going on that needs attention and care. Our daily grind and duties can often make it difficult for us to notice these red flags but I feel most parents instinctively know when something is off. That they might remain in denial or pretend everything is okay out of fear or insecurity is another thing.

I keep saying this over and over again—your children are not your report card as parents. They are not a reflection of your abilities or lack thereof. You're probably the only one who judges yourself harshly for any trouble they are in. Don't let fear of judgement or '*log kya kahenge* (what will people say)?' prevent you from seeking help from counsellors or therapists. The folks whose judgements you are afraid of may be important in your life, but if they stand between you and what your children need, you are better off without them. It has taken me years to understand that shaming has no place in my life. Anyone who points a finger at signs of vulnerability, fear and uncertainty in me or my child deserves to be shown the door out of our lives. What we need and welcome is loving care and if we don't have family to get that from, we find a professional.

There are so many children who are on the neurodivergent spectrum and everyday tasks that are easy for most children may be difficult for them. Neurodiversity (which includes ADHD, autism and Asperger's among other conditions) is not a disorder or disease, it is merely a different wiring of the brain and neurodivergent children have beautiful gifts of creativity, problem solving and imagination to offer the world. It is just that, in a larger system that is oriented to outcomes, productivity, discipline and regimentation, these beautiful brains that flow freely and wildly, feel suffocated.

And then there are children who may have heightened sensitivity to loud sounds, light, repeated movements; things that you might find odd or strange. If that is how your child reacts from a very young age and you don't know what to do, read up on what might be the issue. Chances are your child may be a Highly Sensitive Person or HSP, which is one condition on the neurodivergent spectrum. There is help available for these in the form of reading material, online forums, Facebook groups and communities, specialized childcare and diagnostics, therapy, occupational therapy and counselling. You are not alone. Not in this day and age when we are so connected to each other. Step out of fear and into acceptance. It is not easy, but it is worth it. Our children deserve our best efforts for the simple fact that we chose to have them. To try and make this life as accepting as possible for them, is on us not them.

Normalize seeking professional help in your family

We enter into parenthood with the assumption that all our life before the moment of our child's birth has been preparing us for this journey. And we feel that becoming parents in itself will teach us all we need, we assume that we know better and that we know best. The truth is, we know very little. For a lot of us, our children's birth is a voyage into the land of mists and marshes where the next steps are foggy at best. But all the markers and signposts tell us that we know the way, that we can lead our children into health and success. But parenthood, even though it has existed for years, is like a whole new territory in which it takes some scrambling and falling, some yelling for help and holding on to others' hands to get up and find our way. And that's okay. Don't be misled by the signposting along the way. Feel the drop in your stomach and the terror in your heart to tell you that you are lost and it's time to ask for help.

In some ways I am grateful for my journey from absolute chaos, attempting suicide at nineteen and finally getting into therapy and healing in my thirties. I had to do it alone in the beginning. Friends showed me the way and nudged me, but my family, especially my parents, were lost. They belong to a generation where therapy and seeking help from professionals is for the certifiably insane. Therefore, they had shied away from getting me the help I had obviously needed. Perhaps they were scared, perhaps they didn't know how or maybe they felt that marriage and children would fix me. It didn't. The cost of that delay in finding my way to healing has been immense but the gifts of learning I found along the meandering path to wellness have more than made up for any losses.

I started therapy not very many years ago. Imaad was six years old, I think, and I remember the fuss he kicked up about staying at home, with someone babysitting him, when I went away. The fact that my therapist lived in Delhi made things difficult, but I figured that, if this was how it was going to be for some time, I had to find ways to make this appear very normal. On my first trip to the therapist, I called ahead and told my therapist that Imaad would be accompanying me and asked whether it would be okay if he could wait in the lounge outside while I was in session. My therapist is this great, warm guy who made me feel very welcome from the start. I am forever in debt to the friend who introduced me to him.

On my way to Delhi, I explained to Imaad what therapy was all about and why people needed it. In very simple terms, I explained to him that we need doctors for our bodies when we get hurt, fall sick or break a leg, and we need doctors for our minds and hearts too when we feel sad or lost. And that we were going to one such doctor for Amma because she was feeling lost and sad. He understood that very well. I took toys, colouring books and snacks for him as we did for every outing or trip so that it felt like any other regular outing. When we got there, I was surprised to find that my therapist asked to say hello to Imu. We went in and Imaad was offered a box of colours and a sweet. My therapist and my son have got on very well ever since. Seeking a professional who is warm and friendly for yourself and your child, as and when needed, will go a long way in making you both feel accepted and welcome. It will also take the edge off the nervousness we tend to feel while going into therapy.

Not everyone gets as lucky as I did and after becoming a Life Coach myself, I have met many clients with horror stories of judgemental therapists who made them feel bad about themselves or plied them with drugs before getting to know them well. It can be an exhausting search to find someone who shows compassion and care while dealing with you or your child. Here are some tips that can help:

- Take time and change therapists or counsellors until you find someone who makes you or your child feel safe and invokes trust.

- State your needs clearly for yourself or your child and don't hesitate to ask questions while respecting the professional's boundaries and personal space.

- You can't just telephone therapists at all times unless there's an acute emergency. State your concern or question clearly in a message if you're connected on phone or social media.

- Keep interactions respectful and brief. But if you're confused about something, go back and seek clarifications.

- There are many healing modalities available from traditional psychotherapy to counselling, to medical practitioners, neuro-linguistic programming practitioners and life coaches. See what works best for you, your child or your family Do your research and ask enough questions before you trust someone with yourself, your child and your money.

- Any good practitioner will challenge you to some extent because simply agreeing with everything you say might not always help you. If the practitioner holds space for you or your child with compassion and occasionally challenges you towards growth, they are worth sticking to. If you expect only yes men or women, please know that you can't grow or heal like that. Especially if this is about your child, if a practitioner asks you to make some changes in the way you deal with your child or the home environment, perceiving this suggestion as a personal attack and taking umbrage is not going to help your child. Know that those changes are necessary for your child and make them to whatever extent possible. Taking your parental ego along when seeking help for your child is only going to hurt you both. Leave your ego at home.

- Run from anyone who sounds like the judgemental neighbourhood aunty or uncle. A good practitioner will never be judgemental. They might challenge your perspective but that will hardly be doing so in a shaming way. If your body feels safe in someone's presence, trust your gut and stay to see how things go.

- Be consistent with follow-ups and sessions. Most issues are deep rooted and will not go away quickly. Therapy/counselling/coaching is not magic. All of these take time. Think of these as a long-term investment, while not making it a crutch.

- If it's for your child, you'll be responsible for scheduling, taking your child for the appointments and making your child comfortable with the process. Try and make this as easy as possible for your child with no resentment or a look-I-have-to-do-this-for-you attitude. You're not doing your child a favour; this is something they need. Do not guilt them about this. It will make them hate to go.

- I know this process can be hard with the ten million responsibilities you have. Confide in friends and share your frustrations and worries elsewhere, not with your children. Find a container for your emotions as you go through this process with your children. They can't deal with your problems right now.

- Above everything else, have faith. If you've had it tough as a child, it's not necessary that your child will too and that it will be permanent. Trust in the innate resilience of children and your ability to love them well. Seeking therapy for your children is not a weakness. It is a sign of your commitment to their well-being. You will make it through to the other side. Remember to be gentle with yourself. You've got this.

For the longest time I used to blame myself for my son's emotional issues. I would blame my own volatility and turbulence, my history of being abused, suicidal tendencies and the pain I suffered in my marriage and my ex-husband for everything Imaad and I were going through. It would be wrong to say that I had no responsibility in how the past, certain events and relationships panned out. If we keep blaming ourselves or others, it's as futile as walking up an escalator that is going down. You won't get anywhere. Get off the blame route and take responsibility first for yourself and then for your child. All the while remembering that you will be able to guide and support them to some extent and then they will have to make the rest of the journey on their own, just as you did. Trust that the universe will send them support, just as you found it in unexpected places.

I was thirty-eight when things started falling into place and I finally found a home in my NLP community, The Lightweaver Group, where I found love and wisdom from my teacher, Bhavana Nissima, who is now a dear friend, and acceptance from my friend and fellow coaches in the group. And the journey to this place became possible through countless friends, my siblings, some teachers in school, friends who put opportunities my way, families who took me in when I felt homeless, my therapist and the resources my father shared so kindly so I could learn more. Sometimes getting somewhere can feel like a lifetime of travel and by the time you arrive, you are bone tired and your emotional reserves feel depleted. It is also possible that one destination where we have found succour will not be the end of the road;

nothing ever is. Trust that the gifts of fulfilment will find you
if you remain open to receive and heed the signs that tell you
to listen and learn. Only one thing can stop your growth and
healing, and that is to become closed off and bitter which is
hard not to do because sometimes there's just too much pain.
But keep trying despite the pain. Because, if you try, your child
will notice your efforts and will know that it is possible to heal
and change; the child will have first-hand evidence of the way
you shape your life in interdependence with many others you
encounter on your path. If you remain soft and open, like a
bird that falls so many times but still tries to fly and enjoy the
sky, your child will know that it is possible to emerge from the
shadows of unpleasant life experiences.

My son is open to coaching and learning because I have
practised learning every day in his presence. I put myself into
workshops, courses and retreats until I found my centre. And
while that couldn't have been possible without support and
resources, the fact that I kept trying and changed from the
raging, crying, anxious mess I was to what I am now (still a
bit weird, but mostly cool), has meant that my son witnessed
first-hand the power of possibility and effort. We have easy
discussions about mental health even if these discussions are
sometimes based on memes. I share resources with him and
encourage him to seek coaching or therapy when he is in a
bad place. He has become a little resistant as he has grown
older, but I think that's mostly because teenagers have to rebel
to find their own path. I trust that will happen. It happened to
me too. After years of running from myself, I found a way to
return with love.

Imaad refers to my therapist as the Gentle Fire-Breathing
Dragon and I think he likes that. They get on a call when things
get rough for Imu. I have been labelled the Demon Counsellor
and my work is called Mental-Space Poopology and Never

Let Poo (both, his versions of Mental-Space Psychology and Neuro-Linguistic Programming). I think they're really cool titles! Mental-health awareness and therapy need not always be scary and while you may never be as weird as we are (and that's okay!), you can learn to familiarize yourself with the gift that these processes can be, both for you and your child.

Well-fed children who get good grades and excel in sports are not the only indicators of wellness, health and success. It is also the ability to move their bodies because it gives them joy. It is the ability to stay questioning and curious in a world that is becoming increasingly polarized and closed off. It is the ability to cherish boredom and doing nothing as vital nourishment for the imagination. Above everything else, I feel that health is remaining alive to possibility and care; for self and others. So alive that we remain resilient despite the many pressures of life and bounce back like a dog's tail bounces back no matter how long and how tightly it is restricted. If we are able to give our children this, I believe we have given them the world.

I want to share a delightful poem with you. It defines what education, support and guidance for children means to me. It may be about a teacher and a student, but to me, it is the essence of what our children need most from us.

Mrs Nelson explained how to stand still and listen
to the wind, how to find meaning in pumping gas,
how peeling potatoes can be a form of prayer.

She took questions on how not to feel lost in the dark
After lunch she distributed worksheets
that covered ways to remember your grandfather's
voice.

Then the class discussed falling asleep
without feeling you had forgotten to do something else—
something important—and how to believe
the house you wake in is your home.

This prompted Mrs Nelson to draw a chalkboard
diagram detailing
how to chant the Psalms during cigarette breaks,
and how not to squirm for sound when your own
thoughts
are all you hear; also, that you have enough.

The English lesson was that I am
is a complete sentence.

And just before the afternoon bell, she made the math
equation
look easy. The one that proves that hundreds of
questions,
and feeling cold, and all those nights spent looking
for whatever it was you lost, and one person
add up to something.*

I leave you with a lot of love. My hands in your hands, nose
to nose and looking into your eyes, I say to you, 'I see you. I
see your worry and your strength. I see all that came before
your child and all that will come long after you are gone. Your
presence is a possibility. You are enough, your child is enough.
And you are both loved.'

---

*Modlin, Brad Aaron, 'What You Missed That Day You Were Absent from
Fourth Grade'.

Resources for Children and Parents

Over the years I have read a lot of books and blogs and watched videos on topics that are hard to talk about with kids. I am happy to share these with you. Most of the books mentioned have been authored in India, making them contextually relevant.

Books about our bodies, puberty and sex education for kids

- *The Red Book* by TARSHI for adolescents
- *The Blue Book* by TARSHI for teens (TARSHI books and resources have been a personal favourite since I was a teen myself. Their e-magazine 'In Plainspeak' is a very valuable resource for all things related to sexuality for adults. TARSHI also offers e-courses on sexuality education for beginners and professionals. This is where my journey as a sexuality educator began.)
- *Body Talk* by Anjali Wason

- *My Little Body Book* by Shruti Singhal
- The Menstrupedia Comic (A great resource for boys too)
- *21 Things Every Teen Should Know* by Divya Jalan
- *Pehli Kitaab-Shareer ki Jaankari* by Zubaan Books (This is available in English and three regional languages.)

Books for parents

Most of these are not traditional parenting books but the heartfelt authenticity they hold make them very effective and warm. I highly recommend these for parents.

- *The Yellow Book* by TARSHI (This is a treasure folks!)
- *All You Need Is Love* by Shelja Sen
- *My Daughters' Mum* by Natasha Badhwar
- *Immortal For a Moment* by Natasha Badhwar
- *Parenting Without Power Struggles* by Susan Stiffelmen
- *The Reluctant Mother* by Zehra Naqvi (This book is written by a very dear friend. It is an essential read to understand the strenuous side of being a parent and life in general. A great resource for men to understand their partners better if the partners are preparing for motherhood or are mothers already.)

Some online resources I love

- The Hands-Free Revolution (Blog)
- Kristina Kuzmic's videos
- Agents of Ishq (This is my favourite place to find videos, articles and blogs on everything from consent,

sex and sex ed to pornography. Created by the amazing Paromita Vohra, AOI is a great place where you can watch and share videos with your older kids.)

- The PANTS Project UK
- Komal (It is very sensitively made animated short film on child sexual abuse that you can watch with your kids and use as a reference point to begin conversations. Available in Hindi and English.)
- Full Stop (It is a very powerful video every parent will benefit from. I use it as a starting point for conversations in workshops.)

Happy reading and watching. Wisdom is in knowing that we can never know enough.

Acknowledgements

It is my firm belief that we create nothing alone, neither our successes nor our failures. Who we are and what we can become are threads of multiple possibilities that weave in and out of us, connecting us to family, friends, ancestors and events that happened to us, around us.

I am forever grateful to my parents Israr Khan and Saeeda Naqvi for giving me the space and resources to take my time meandering without getting anywhere. My siblings Asad, Saba and Sadaf have been my fiercest supporters. My gratitude for them and my siblings in law Aisha, Iqbal and Kamal who have been my cheerleaders. My son Imaad has brought out both the best and worst in me and holding them together is what makes me the mother I am. This book is our journey. Thank you Imu. The kids in my life are the reason this book exists. My love to my nephews, niece and all the kids who generously call me Reema Aunty.

My Bajis at home are the reason I can write and work without worrying about the household. Thank you Razia Baji and Gudiya Baji. Fluffy love to my non-human family for never letting me feel lonely.

I have been blessed with the most amazing friends one could wish for. My friends Bianca Ghose, Zehra Naqvi and Pranav Sharma have supported not just me but also this book. My friends and in many ways mentors, Amita Malhotra and Rajesh Lalwani are the home where my journey back to purpose began. Thank you both. The idea for this book came from my friend, Surabhi Baijal who first suggested that I convert my conversations with Imaad into a book. I am glad I listened to her.

My friend and teacher, Bhavana Nissima has encouraged me endlessly with her belief in my capabilities. My friends Neha Chaturvedi and Semeen Ali have kept me sane and laughing through very tough times in the last two years. I thank them all. My love to my friends from Agra for adopting me and Imaad. My love to my college friends who continue to remind me of the Reema they first knew. Then there are friends I cannot name because they are no longer a part of my life. But for their contribution in my journey, I thank them.

Gratitude for my high school English teachers Poorna Verma and Vandana Ghosh. They encouraged my love for reading and writing. Love and light to my Lightweaver Community; you are my comfort. My Facebook community has cheered me on endlessly; my thanks to them.

My sincere thanks to Rana Safvi who pushed me to pitch my book. And to Kanishka Gupta, my wonderful agent. He made the whole process a breeze for me. Many thanks to my editor Gurveen Chaddha for her patience and kindness.

Lastly, my thanks to my late Mamu, Kazim Naqvi, who told me I would write a book one day when I was twelve. I miss you Mamujaan.